CONTEMPORARY MANITOBA WRITERS
New Critical Studies

CONTEMPORARY MANITOBA WRITERS
New Critical Studies

Kenneth James Hughes, Editor

Turnstone Press

Cover photo credits:
Top row, left to right: SANDRA BIRDSELL (Gerald Brydon), PATRICK FRIESEN (Marijke Friesen). Second row: ROBERT KROETSCH (Marilyn Morton), WAYNE TEFS (Alison Gillmor). Third row: KRISTJANA GUNNARS (W.C. Christie), DENNIS COOLEY (Dana Cooley), BIRK SPROXTON (Elaine McRoberts). Bottom row: DAVID ARNASON (Horst Siegler), GEORGE AMABILE (Gordon MacKenzie), CAROL SHIELDS (Jeff DeBooy).

Turnstone Press
607-100 Arthur Street
Winnipeg, Manitoba
Canada R3B 1H3

Turnstone Press gratefully acknowledges the assistance of the Manitoba Arts Council and the Canada Council.

This book was printed and bound in Canada by Hignell Printing Limited for Turnstone Press.

"13 Ways of Looking at Pat Friesen" by Wayne Tefs was previously published, in slightly different form, in *Border Crossings*, Vol. 7, No. 2 (April 1988).

Canadian Cataloguing in Publication Data

Main entry under title:

Contemporary Manitoba writers: new critical studies

ISBN 0-88801-152-0

1. Canadian literature (English) - Manitoba - History and criticism.* 2. Canadian literature (English) - 20th century - History and criticism.* I. Hughes, Kenneth James, 1932-

PS8131.M2C66 1990 C810.9'97127 C90-097197-5
PR9198.2.M2C66 1990

For my daughters,
Dodie and Clara

CONTENTS

ix Preface / *Kenneth James Hughes*

1 Amabile's "First Light": Decentering and Disruption / *Kenneth James Hughes*

31 Arnason's Irony and Vision / *Margaret Sweatman*

54 13 Ways of Looking at Pat Friesen / *Wayne Tefs*

64 "Drawing /in": Wholeness and Dislocation in the Work of Kristjana Gunnars / *Judith Owens*

79 Robert Kroetsch's *Seed Catalogue*: The Deconstruction of the Meta-narrative of the Cowboy / *David Arnason*

93 Sandra Birdsell's *Agassiz Stories*: Speaking the Gap / *Charlene Diehl-Jones*

110 *Figures on a Wharf*: Shaping Things to Come / *Birk Sproxton*

131 Decentering the Text: Transgression and Dialogue in Dennis Cooley's *Bloody Jack* / *Debbie D'Aoust*

146 Notes on Birk Sproxton's *Headframe:* / *Dennis Cooley*

163 From "Dying for Love" to "Mrs. Turner": Narrative Control in Stories by Carol Shields / *Herb Weil*

177 Contributors

Preface

Kenneth James Hughes

"It is easy to see that we are living in a time of rapid and radical social change. It is much less easy to grasp the fact that such change will inevitably affect the nature of those academic disciplines that both reflect our society and help to shape it."

So begins Terence Hawkes' Preface to that remarkable series of New Accents books by Methuen, of which Hawkes is the General Editor. These Methuen books helped bring home to a large Anglo-American audience in English Departments the "bad news" that they were (and still are) hopelessly out of date in the light of

a) the deepening social, economic, pedagogical and general intellectual crisis;
b) the response to that crisis in the form of a postmodern multi-headed critical discourse Hydra of Russian, Czech, Polish, German, French, Italian and other origins.

In different degrees at different historical times the world has been experienced as in a state of change, so much so that the word "rapid" (as in "rapid change") must be considered in relation to local norms in different phases of history. Nonetheless, change can be considered to be of two fundamentally different kinds:

a) That kind of incremental and quantitative change which occurs without bringing into consciousness and question the fundamental principles or presuppositions on which a culture is based. People become so habituated to these presuppositions that they erroneously assume them to be permanent facts of an unchanging "nature." They fail to see them for what they are: culturally constructed presuppositions that are socially reproduced in conscious minds by concealed levels of key discourse codes (e.g. verbal, visual, monetary) as they circulate in everyday life. These changes are relatively easy to assimilate since they do not challenge the socially produced presuppositions of the mind and culture.
b) The truly revolutionary qualitative periods of change. These periods unearth the fundamental presuppositions which underlie thought and which validate or authorize it. Such an unearthing declares the presuppositions to be cultural and historical rather than natural. This occurred between the archaic Greeks and the classical Greeks, between medieval mythos culture and the 17th-century secular scientific culture, and between the latter and the as yet undefined emergent system which it has been the awesome task of our violent 20th century to construct.

The periods of revolutionary change I call periods of infraparadigm change, as opposed to the simpler and easier incremental quantitative or metaparadigm change. Infraparadigm periods of change are particularly painful and complex because there no longer exists any agreement among people about the fundamental foundations or presuppositions of knowledge. Yet, somehow, the infraparadigm presuppositions of the old system of knowledge must be deconstructed, while the as yet unknown new system of knowledge must be constructed. The overlap between the presuppositions of the contradictory old and new systems ensures that the everyday world of experience in such dramatic and extended periods of change becomes very complex and problematic. This is because the historical process involves de-programming minds and re-programming them simultaneously, all in a context in which

a) the work of the world must go on, and
b) we do not yet know what the new program should fully look like.

For this reason, the realm of literature along with everything else becomes complex and problematic, with the consequence that activities in these realms must also become very complex and problematic. The new criticism must somehow variously:

a) deal with the old literary discourse;
b) deal with the old literary critical discourse;
c) attempt to make its own inherited critical discourse (which was designed to handle the old literary discourse) fit the new literary discourse (which it was not designed to do);
d) take account also of the complexities of the empirical world itself (the "real" as I call it in my following essay) as the matrix of the new.

Some of the texts in this collection may seem relatively complex. I offer no apology for this. The world we live in is no simple place, and it does not lend itself to simple treatment, at least not to the simple-minded kind of treatment that the old and easily read sort of literary critical discourse now seems to have been.

I see this text as the first of a series of critical essays on Prairie writing, though not a series done by me. Certainly such a series is needed. May my successors do justice to those I could not include here (but would have loved to have done), may they encourage more new critical writers because we need them, may they have the same happy and unproblematical relations with their contributors, and may they above all else be lucky enough to have the always generous help of Turnstone's Marilyn Morton, Paula Kelly, Manuela Dias and Patricia Sanders.

Amabile's "First Light": Decentering and Disruption

Kenneth James Hughes

First Light

I

Birdsong. A few scattered notes
that flare and melt in the dark
even before the vague streets and parks
begin to invade the night's brief amnesia.

Leafless trees, the moth-eaten rug
of dead grass in the park, the empty
streets, the dust, the first
bus bunting its blunt head
like a whale through the quiet . . .

and over the shadowy hulk
of St. Augustine's Church, a full
moon fades like the ghost
of a shocked infant
sucked from the nipple by a storm.

* * * *

In the empty
Safeway
parking lot
after a long night

in a black
depression
filled with rain

water, oil
refines the drab light
to a garish rainbow—
chartreuse, magenta, peacock blue

then the painful
fiesta of dawn
begins

and suddenly it's clear
that I am a part of the morning
the part that watches
while it burns.

* * * *

Mystery gives way
to belief and belief
gives way to knowledge
and the small teeth of the mind
grind on, but safety is nothing
more than time disguised
as a clock. The season
hesitates, the air revives
old failures, old loves
that hover like fragrant shadows
or cool wings, as we cruise
without too much control
toward what we're told
are more refined adventures.

* * * *

In the beginning there was always
(though we left it like a shed skin
to dry at the back of the cave
of the mind) the need
to know what had happened before us.

Believing what we thought we held
in memory, we began
to obey imperatives: Fate
Gods, Biology, dream work, stories
about the star at the core
of an apple, the sudden shift
of light in animal eyes.

> *To begin is to enter always*
> *days that have already come*
> *to pass: visions*
> *eaten without salt by fanatics,*
> *milestones, codes, epiphanies:*
> *collapsed stars in the mind. . . .*

When mayflies tumble
out of the sun to litter
the sidewalks and pavements
of lakeside resorts;
when comets with tighter schedules
than buses or trains
return from the limitless night
we lived in before
we learned how to scratch
pictures on the walls
of caves, insights
flare through a husk
of selves and the light
they admit reveals
as it fades
a shadow dance
a slipped encounter soft as rain.

* * * *

Fragrance of cedar on the lake-
shore breeze, like the kiss
of an innocent prince, revives
that sleepy paradise we sometimes dream, just
before dawn.
My heartbeat shifts
to overtime. I need to grow
more skin.

* * * *

Rhinoceros, I love your folded
argument, your sullen will.
Birds flutter and peck
at your back. Your ears
twitch. Your thick
blood slows down in the sun. What
do you feel, I wonder.
What do you think
of the fleet beasts
with delicate horns
who dance by all day
at the edge
of your stuffy daydreams?

In Nairobi, the sliced
organized bodies
of other breathers
ooze pink liquids
under cellophane
and refrigerated music.

Soothe me, leaf eater.
Lend me your sense of time.

* * * *

Steaming tea in a glass cup on the desk.
Light is the Lion that comes down
to drink . . . I admire those words, the risk
they take, like saying, "my mind is grass, brown
or green in the sun of centuries, in Africa
where human life begins . . ." and yet
they seem far fetched. Morning traffic
steams and crawls like a herd while sun-dogs threaten
the body with such vivid cold
it's hard to see how the Cree, with their simple flames
and hides, could survive it. And what of the lion, sold
into sleep at the Zoo? Is he the same
final consumer clothed in scruffy gold
who came to drink, and cleared the waterhole?

II

Chicken fat sizzles on propane barbecues.
The river shoulders its huge
indifference
through crumbling lips
of dirt. It's not the world I knew
as a child with one leg
in a red wagon
pushing hard, faster
and faster until the ball
of my foot just grazed the sidewalk, flying
toward the great white sun
where I could shout
my unrepeatable name and explode.

* * * *

Approaching escape
velocity I came
down with a case of viral pneumonia.

The priest made a rare house call
with his book, his candles
and his fair-weather face.

Grief and loss and fear of the cold
erased my common sense. After the syllables
running like a smooth betrayal

into wrinkled sheets
there was the old silence
harmless, and without degrees.

Profit continued
to activate the glands
of a wartime economy.

* * * *

I lay on my daybed in the darkened living room
feeling my thighs melt from their bones.

A horde of minute barbarians ate my lungs.
I tried half-heartedly to eat them back.

Then I slipped away into soft countries.
Centuries later, sparrows

quarrelled in the first leaves and the sun
glowed through stained windowshades

that looked like parchment
maps of *The New World*.

* * * *

Thistles don't care.

When I came
weakly into the brisk
light of May, they

were prickly and stubborn.
Lilacs were nearly the same

colour but they were kind.
The wind played with my hair
then pushed me over.
I rubbed my eyes, got back
up on my feet. I dreamed
there were no animals left
in the city. Even the rats
had climbed at night
on hawsers over a slack tide
onto the last freighters.

I wanted to travel
too. I envied heroes
but I'd lost my sense
of adventure. I took

to lounging on the porch
with *The Hunchback*
of Notre Dame. Clouds
went by. The neighbourhood
alcoholic sang
me a blurry song about Garibaldi.
It felt as though thin bandages
had come loose and sailed
away from his broken heart.
Lilacs bloomed in the dooryard.
Only my worried mother gave a damn.

* * * *

Strength returned
and made me normal
just in the nick
of time. I learned
how to stand
by. My heart
passed every test
got carried away
happy to spend
its life in a crib of rules.

* * * *

Geometry seduced me.
I loved its desert of abstract
events, the coolness
the invisible
points, the lines
and axioms. The smell
of the sea seduced me too.
The sun warming old wood, old shells
the slow reach
and retreat of the tides
the rainbow mist
blown up over the rocks
by the waves, the wet
streets, the cobblestones and weeds.

Then I had this dream:

I've been walking for hours
on a desolate road. The dust
has caked on my feet. I don't
know why I'm here, or where
I'm going. All around me
the trees have closed
their leaves and daylight
drains from the sky. It takes
the heat of my blood with it.
Then, where the road curves
I see him dancing, a silly
man with a grease paint smile,
in the white suit of a clown.
Fat stars—yellow, orange, green and red—
pulse from his costume.
I take his hand. We leave
the road, laughing
through dead leaves that breathe
comforting news about the night
that cannot invade us. Soon

we are cosmic acrobats, leaping
from the spin of one galactic
fingerprint to the next
higher and higher, until I see
that his eyes are blank
as ice when he laughs.
His teeth are arranged
in rows like the teeth of a shark.

III

this is what it means
to love the world
more than the world deserves

the fear
ladder
of water
skin
breath

* * * *

Perhaps the mind is nothing
but an oscillating
dream, interrupted
by apnea whenever it starts
to remember what must fade
with the dawn. On the street
fistfuls of dusty noise
blow it askew. It invents
revised geographies
and when it stops to think
a glimpse of everything
at once closes it down.
Fog swirls in the wet park
and even sunlight fails to clear
the barely breatheable air. What
can it do after that
but wake up and sing?

* * * *

Under the logic of ledgers and sleights of thought, archetypes open their wings. Where does it come from, this halting voice that takes direction out of the random night?

above the black-boned
hanging lamp's
river misted
hills in milky glass
large petals
of light float
on the ceiling, turning
in the slow moving air
over the rise
and fall of mixed
vernaculars, the steamy ghosts
of soup, the candle's
aura breathing
in the wall's red silk
brocade like the wings
of a sleepy dragon
this work day
evening at *The Wu*
Li and I think
back over an afternoon
full of words
how the pencil whispered
and scraped, how the blade
skimmed off a ribbon
of rosewood edged in white
which broke as it fell
into small fans

* * * *

Sometimes history changes key and soars. Sometimes it sits there like a damaged animal. Who knows what madness commends itself purely on the authority of an absent-hearted smile?

* * * *

the sagging roofs
and doorways of abandoned houses
doze in the heat
of a small yellow star

in the yard, glass
fragments glitter
on a buckled flagstone walk
among the fiercely white
bones of catfish and carp

the hard shadow
of a bird cuts
across a trapezoid
of light in the pantry

* * * *

Keep the trucks humming and rolling
over hunched black hills
into the valleys and across the plains.

(in the West
a swamp of decayed light
eats the horizon)

Keep the world from changing while we sleep.

* * * *

Ambition itself consumed the pleasures of dawn. Out of lingering doubts that prompt the soul to give itself up in the shadow of mountains, I came with my packages and small change. Nothing I learned from the backward valleys poured me a glass of sunlight when I sat down to break my fast in the empty kitchen.

* * * *

I was busy changing gears
pumping a squeaky bike
through the soft light before dark
when the forgotten sweetness
of lilacs opened and spread
all the summers of my life around me

somewhere
in that inexhaustible
season a child
held a broken cup
up to the sun

* * * *

ice cracks in the glass. a universe
of molecules rearranges itself: water
carbon dioxide, vodka, lime juice and particles
of dust from the breeze that comes in
through the window, softly
prescribing autumn, a turning
at which it is appropriate (though perhaps risky)
to make resolutions:
don't drink too much, but give
your arteries a daily sluice. buy exotic
tobaccos but don't inhale before dark.
work the large muscle groups, especially the heart
once a day but only to the slightest
burn. don't persist or persevere.
just do what needs to be done. avoid
christmas like the plague. drive out
under the sky and sit there
quietly among the ticks and fumes
of the cooling motor, thinking
of nothing, letting your mask
of words dissolve in the effortless night.

go home and sit down by the fireside's light.
convince your self-image to jump in the river
and put a stop to this thing you have about final manoeuvres.

Operating Assumption

Even a modest analysis of Amabile's new and hitherto unpublished long poem (a significant global-spatial and temporal number of 365 lines long) cannot be realized in the space available here. In the interests of making a maximum use of this space, I shall therefore begin with the heuristic (fictional working) assumption that the majority of people in this culture have been inscribed with the codes of classical English poetic discourse, which they assume to be "natural," and that they would therefore prefer (either secretly or openly) a Shakespearean sonnet to the apparent confusions of, say, Eliot's "The Wasteland" and Amabile's "First Light." If I am wrong in this assumption, my preliminary analysis will have outlined a situation in the near past rather than in the immediate present, so all will not be lost.

Some Megaconcepts

Because analysis always requires an ideological framework, I shall begin my discussion with the megaconcepts of imaginary, symbolic, and real.

The Real

Simply stated, the real refers to the whole of nature and culture as "objects" of human knowledge. Only a god, it is said, can occupy a transcendental viewing post outside of nature and culture. This means that nothing can be known about the real in our day except through the codes of the symbolic or the imaginary. The problem immediately emerges as to whether the present dominant symbolic is appropriate to present needs.

The Symbolic

The symbolic refers to all the discourse codes (written, mathematicized, spoken, sung, danced, gestured, etc.) that make up the dominant discursive formation or symbolic in a culture. Up to the Renaissance in England the dominant discursive formation or symbolic was the mythos- or religion-"centered" feudal one. At the heart of that discursive formation was a transcendent being, who was nonetheless culturally centered both as the source and final validation for all knowledge (mediated through the church, of course).

Feudal vs. Real Symbolic

In the 17th century a decisive battle occurred in England (it had been lost in Italy) between remnants of the feudal symbolic or discursive formation and the Newtonian/Cartesian realist symbolic which replaced it. This realist symbolic decentered the feudal Christian God and banished him. The new realist-based conceptual universe had no room for him. The new realist symbolic denied the validity of feudal knowledge, much of which it transformed into its own secular terms and uses. For example, intellect as transcendental site (and sight) of the new autonomous bourgeois subject, or "I" (and "eye": male and propertied only), which looked at the world in secular terms as object, replaced the "intellectus" of the feudal symbolic, the means by which the medieval few could acquire anagogical knowledge (the highest of the four feudal levels of knowledge) of God.

This bourgeois intellect, or I, came into existence with the new realist symbolic. It became the source and validation of secular knowledge in the new Newtonian/Cartesian science system. (The Latin *scientia*, or science, meant theology, the science of the knowledge of God, not nature, for medievals. The latter was secondary knowledge.) This symbolic and "I" put the bourgeois subject into linear teleological history conceived of as progress. It inscribed in new realist minds the meta-narrative of progress as a mental ideological framework. It transformed the highway from the misery of earth to the heaven of after-life in the feudal mythos symbolic into a secular utopian heaven on earth, set sometime in the future (an ever-receding future, it seems). This meta-narrative of mercantile capitalism licensed imperial expansion and racism, and ultimately it produced industrial capitalism. Utopian literature emerged everywhere in the 17th century, but by the end of the 19th century and into the 20th century, the dominant serious literary mode was dystopian or pessimistic, marking the decline of the meta-narrative of progress.

All these historical features become problematic in the 20th century, and they emerge as highly condensed problematics that Amabile thematizes in the semantic fragments that interweave the text of "First Light." The fragmentation of the Amabile text therefore reflects the collapse of the meta-narrative of progress and linear history (without the pessimism), as well as the collapse of the realist discursive formation or symbolic, which still remains dominant all these years later. Amabile's text itself constitutes an attack on the realist symbolic from out of the imaginary.

The Imaginary

Creating the discourse forms of a discursive formation or symbolic means setting up conceptual boundaries in the mental and social realms of knowledge. These discourse forms put boundaries around concepts of things that are undifferentiated in the real. Conceptualization in the symbolic therefore constitutes the real according to its own presuppositions. This causes people to see the real in terms of the symbolic through psychogenetically inscribed realist codes, which on their other side serve as sociogenetic codes to define a whole civilization. However, in this process of constituting the real through conceptualization in the symbolic, not all the characteristics of the real may fit the conceptual framework of the symbolic. The symbolic therefore represses certain features of the real and (because of its ideological presuppositions or blinkers) persons inscribed with the codes of the symbolic will not be able to "see" everything about the real.

This realm of the repressed outside of the real as defined by the symbolic is the imaginary. The imaginary proves to be the only possible source of new knowledge, hence its function as the site from which attacks on the realist symbolic or discursive formation emerge in attempts to change or replace it.

Amabile's "First Light" marks an attempt from the imaginary to deconstruct the realist symbolic, an attempt to subvert the codes of both realist poetic discourse as well as those of the larger realist discursive formation or symbolic.

Normative Realism

The realist poetic discourse (with parallels in music, visual discourse, physics, etc.) has been under attack since the early 20th century, yet it nonetheless still remains as the normative poetic discourse for most people. For heuristic (working) purposes, it will be considered so here, subject to one strict condition: that "normative" does not become confused with "normal" (in the privileging sense) or "natural." To consider realism natural means that the realist symbolic would have to be identical with the real, but that is the ideological notion which Amabile very correctly attacks.

Attacking Realism

Amabile belongs to a 20th-century poetic movement (with more than poetry involved), stretching from modernism into postmodernism. It emerges out of the imaginary as an actually new poetic discourse which forms part of a potentially new discursive formation or symbolic.

The Dominant Realist Symbolic

For ease of reference, any of Shakespeare's sonnets will serve as an example of realist poetic discourse. (The poetic level I am talking about goes beyond the conventional "literary" distinctions into Neoclassical, Romantic, Victorian, because it lies behind those distinctions on a different level.) Roughly put, a typical Shakespearean sonnet will have:

a) 14 lines
b) 10-syllable lines
c) normative iambic pentameter rhythms
d) normative syntax
e) end rhyme (not with blank verse)
f) three-part linear structure
(beginning, middle, end)
g) three-part statement of theme, development, conclusion (equilibrium, disequilibrium, equilibrium)
h) monology (a single logic guides the way to the conclusion from behind the text)
i) monological closure which affirms a single set of (controlling) values.

Amabile from the Imaginary

Amabile's much larger text has:

a) 365 lines
b) variable line lengths
c) variable rhythms without norm
d) two kinds of fragmented syntax
e) some near rhyme
f) three-part structure: non-linear
(It begins, has a middle and an end as a material structure, but thematically it does not work in the linear way.)
g) no guiding monology
h) no monological closure and no affirmation of a single or specific set of values, though it does in general affirm life.

Disrupting Realist Codes

There is nothing accidental about this point-by-point Amabile deconstruction of classic realist poetic discourse, as we shall see with his simultaneous deconstruction of the plain prose discourse, which functions rather as a meta-discourse.

Plain Prose Discourse

Throughout the 16th and into the 17th century, coincident with the rise of the centralized national state, some important people doubted the expressive potential of "the English language" (which means that southern English dialect among dialects, connotation among connotations, the dialect as connotation that would be privileged as the denotative "the" English language). "The" language of learning then was Latin. By 1660, that southern English dialect had been transformed from the plain prose discourse of the London Puritan preachers, lawyers and merchants in sermons and contracts to become "the" language (or rather discourse) of truth, soon validated by the new Scientific Royal Society of London to replace Latin. As the dominant prose non-fiction ideological form (along with it came the prose fiction novel) of science, plain prose non-fiction became a meta-discourse that subordinated to it all other verbal discourses, including poetry. Significantly, Amabile inserts short sections of plain prose into his text. This act:

a) reverses the 17th-century subordination of poetry to prose by deliberately introducing a little prose in a lot of poetry, textually subordinating prose to poetry;
b) sets up a marked contrast between the expressive powers of his multi-levelled poetic discourse and the expressive poverty of the semantically uni-dimensional prose meta-discourse.

Dominant Codes: Social Production & Reproduction

To understand how disruption works in "First Light," we need to start with the social production and reproduction of the human subject. A reading of Vygotsky's work would outline the complex way in which a culture works as a productive and reproductive process to produce human subjects (not without stiff resistance from the young). But space limitations preclude the pursuit of Vygotsky here (he transcends the ideological limitations of Piaget).

Winston Churchill says somewhere that we make buildings and buildings make us. This means that cultural discourse forms are inscribed inside us as coded patterns which make up the mind of the subject, a mind shaped by the dominant cultural symbolic. This mind gets imposed on top of the biological brain (which in fact is three brains) in the production of the human subject. Such codes circulate throughout a culture, and do so through habituating use by humans in the ritual processes of daily life. So inscribed, people commonly think that they freely speak these codes, and as long as they believe this, the codes can reproduce themselves behind the operations of the semantically preoccupied surface awareness of the people using them. Only some major disruption in the real (or in the codes of the realist symbolic which they mistake for the real) can break this circulation and challenge the daily social reproduction of the codes of the symbolic. (A year in the round huts of a native tribe would cure people in the west of their socially reproduced assumption that buildings are rectilinear structures by nature, just as a careful analysis of the tribal language would reveal the cultural, not natural, fact of language.)

Decentering the "I"

The circulating discourse forms that both support and embody the realist discursive formation or symbolic have served to socially reproduce the bourgeois concept of self as a unified ego coming out of the 17th century. To decenter the tattered remnants of that concept and operating assumption (which was Freud's enterprise in part) requires (in addition to changes in social practices in general) a dislocation of the socially reproductive codes of the realist discursive formation or symbolic. Amabile's attack on the realist codes disrupts those codes as an aspect of the ego decentering process, which must finally occur on the psychogenetic level of the subject because of sociogenetic changes in the larger society, themselves produced in large part through human activity in modern and postmodern cultures.

The Problematic "I"

A survey of the personal pronouns and their semantic contexts in "First Light" will reveal an ecologically and morally concerned Amabile creating a persona like himself, one who oscillates between a problematic and half-decentered (hence fragmented, rather than unified) "I," and a universal but strictly historical species being "we." This oscillation proves symptomatic of an emergent and increasingly global centered community of interest. The half-decentered, postmodern REFRACTED "I" stands in stark contrast to the centered anarchist-verging-on-nihilist younger and violent Amabile, the REFLECTED "I" found in the earlier personae of the brutal but brilliant anti-elegies on the death of his father and brother respectively.

Fragmentation

The key characteristic of "First Light" is fragmentation on both the levels of poetic discourse that were particularized above:

semantic plane	(conceptual meaning levels)
plane of expression	(syntax, tone levels, etc.)

Fragmentation also characterizes both the micro-level and macro-level of the text:

textual three parts and part divisions

---

signs to sentences

Macro-Division Boundary Space Function

The space between parts I and II, and II and III, allow a leap back in geo-political, sociological, psychological and historical space and time to early youth in New Jersey from the Winnipeg, Manitoba present of the text. The second permits a return to the Winnipeg-based cosmic present.

The boundary spaces between the units of the three parts allow spatial and temporal leaps back to the beginning of life on earth through the arrival of humans, references to paleolithic cave discourse, and spatial, temporal, cultural leaps from Manitoba to its own Cree past, and across to present-day Africa.

Both these spaces disrupt realist notions of linear, cohesive, coherent monological texts, but Amabile works skilfully to create that illusion of fragmentation without lapsing into the kind of simple incoherence that any fool can write.

Disruption: On the Level of Line

On the level of line this fragmentation technique produces powerful semantic meaning, as we see in the two lines:

> that I am a part of the morning
> the part that watches (lines 30-31)

"Morning" in the first line above serves as a micrometonym of macrometonymic nature, a spatial and temporal part for the whole. The gap at the end of the first line therefore makes the line speak of the human, literally (on certain levels), as a part of nature in the quite pre-modern manner of the archaic Greeks and Medievals. This happens because of the sudden semantic silence at the end of the line, which works as a "focat" (a "focusing category" which puts the focus on a specific semantic area). But the next line renews the semantic development, and introduces the very opposite historical Cartesian view of the human subject separated from nature as:

subject viewer	——>	viewed object
(part that watches)		(the object of the gaze)

(This subject/object split came at a key 17th-century historical phase in the conversion of feudal property into the alienable private property of the bourgeoisie.) The point here is not that the second line qualifies the first, or only qualifies the first, but that in a very economical way, and with great clarity, it puts these two historical, philosophical, and economic views of nature side by side to begin to unfold the secrets of the alienated, fragmented, and problematic present.

Reading Realist Codes

A brief outline of saccadic movement and the stochastic process will help me make a few important points about focats and the precisely ambiguous semantic process between the lines in "First Light" that I have just outlined.

When we read a printed plain prose non-fiction text, the use there of so-called "correct" linear syntax in the relatively few standard forms of syntax employed by the realist writer (and the habituation to them by the reader—the reader in an "educated" home has heard about half a million sentences by the age of five) causes a repression of awareness in the reader of the plane of expression, focusing concentration on the monological and uni-dimensional semantic or conceptual meaning of the lines. Prose non-fiction lines of equal length stretch in a repeated, uniform military order across the page from top to bottom, like a Guards Regiment on parade (as in the lines you are presently reading). This repression and foregrounding process allows the plain prose meta-discourse to silently reproduce itself in the human subject (noun) as it subjects (verb) the human subject (noun) to its codes. Unless the text uses specialized and unfamiliar signs (which themselves can disrupt), a competent reader will get a "massage" as she proceeds through a fast unproblematical decoding of the uni-dimensional semantic plane. (Various strategies in my text here are designed to prevent massaging.) "Massage" refers to the comforting agreement of identity between the expectations prompted by the inner inscribed realist codes in the human subject and the incoming repressed realist plane of expression of the text, with its single monological, linear and foregrounded semantic level.

With some differences that mark off classical poetic discourse from non-fiction prose, the equality of line length, the normative rhythm, syntax and so on, will in degrees produce a similar effect of agreement between the classical codes in the outer poetic object and the inscribed inner realist poetic codes.

In both cases, the eyes with their foveal and peripheral vision look at the text and start reading in order to send data to the mind. The realist inscribed mind decodes that data and reacts to it as a feedback system, telling the eyes what to do next.

Saccadic Movement, Stochastic Process & Estrangement

Because of the seemingly unproblematic character of a non-fiction prose text (it is, in fact, highly problematical as it shows when it gets disrupted by alien signs to reveal its inscribed or constructed character), and because of the relatively unproblematic surface reading of classical poetic discourse (again finally problematical), it is easy to come to the conclusion that human eyes simply scan lines in an unbroken continuous fashion. In fact, they proceed in a hopping fashion as peripheral vision gives way to foveal vision in a process called the saccadic movement across the lines of a text.

The saccadic movement is related to the stochastic process, which works in the following way: foveal and peripheral vision start reading a prose non-fiction text and send preliminary coded data back to the realist inscribed mind. That data produces the primary alienation effect as the mind distinguishes the normative plain prose discourse from other visual possibilities in the empirical world (looking at plain prose in a text is not looking at a car, a loved one, etc.). On the basis of the skimpiest of realist compatible data, the realist mind makes a stochastic leap (a guess) and immediately declares a likely realist prose non-fiction text to be such. It then proceeds in the expectation of receiving further confirming data from foveal and peripheral vision (an old animal-level survival mechanism). If, however, the foveal and peripheral vision send data back unfriendly to the inner realist codes, the realist mind must immediately cancel its hasty stochastic judgement or conclusion and proceed to test the data against other neurally inscribed patterns in search of re-cognition.

If the early data from the eyes to the mind suggests a Shakespearean sonnet (or suggests those linear, generic ancestors to the Amabile poem, Wordsworth's "The Prelude" and Tennyson's "Locksley Hall" and its sequel), then the mind will make another stochastic leap to conclude that further data will match its own realist inscribed classical poetic codes. This judgement marks a secondary-level estrangement effect. The secondary classical poetic estrangement effect distinguishes the classical poetic discourse from prose non-fiction, whose primary estrangement effect distinguishes the looking at prose from looking at a garden, cars and so on.

If the mind has yet again made too sudden a stochastic leap, and if it finds that it has been looking at Eliot's "Prufrock" poem or the Amabile poem, not Shakespeare's sonnet (the plays are something else), it must once more reverse its judgement to produce a tertiary estrangement effect that distinguishes the early Eliot or Amabile poems from the classical poetic discourse, as well as from the plain prose non-fiction discourse. At the same time, the firmly inscribed realist mind must conclude because of its inner realist codes that the Amabile poem is nonsense, a clear sign of the poetic degeneracy of our times in relation to those wonderful times in the past when Mr. Wordsworth and Mr. Tennyson had classical poetic standards, and wrote what good solid realist minds could read with no difficulty. Alternatively, the realist mind must learn "to see" anew in a different way without its realist codes. It must learn the new codes.

Since the circulating realist codes of the realist discursive formation or symbolic are the only support the centered bourgeois ego has for the illusion of autonomy (outside of wealth and power over others), an awareness that these codes are not natural comes as a profound shock, one which shatters the very notion of the autonomous self. Nonetheless, to understand the tertiary-level estranged poetic discourse requires that the realist reader:

a) must learn about his realist inscriptions;
b) must learn that those inscriptions do not have a lot of survival value in a drastically changed culture for which there has been no precedent;
c) must learn that his (in fact always problematic) notion of a unified "I" has been socially reproduced behind his back by those circulating realist codes (supported by the related codes of perspectival realist visual discourse and tonal music, etc.). He must learn that those bad dreams and confusions he has been having lately derive from the collapsing of the realist symbolic and his sense of a unified, autonomous self;
d) must learn that instead of the passive MASSAGING from realist (very quietly active and authoritarian) discourses,

he must look, listen, and feel the MESSAGING on both planes and all the levels of the tertiary-level estrangement text and its new poetic discourse, a messaging coming from the imaginary;

e) must learn that, above all, once he has inscribed himself with the basic codes of the new poetic discourse, he must participate (with the author) in the construction of the "meanings" he himself generates out of the text, meanings that the text makes possible, which he must share with others. This sharing is not in the interests of generating a monological meaning (which kills the text), but in order to gain an orientation in the confusing midst of a whole western civilization and symbolic in the process of massive transition;

f) must learn that without this very active participation, a tertiary-level estrangement text will not work to communicate meaning. Without reader participation, the text is truly nonsense. It exists, but its authentic existence lies not in its being as object, but in its becoming in an active dialectical relationship of process with the reader;

g) must learn that this relationship is not a trivial affair, but the central aporia or problematic of western civilization during its present transition
   i) from the separated and static subject/object relations of the 17th-century Newtonian/Cartesian realist discursive formation or symbolic
   ii) into the 20th-century process orientation of a new and emergent discursive formation or symbolic that requires the active participation of all in its construction (in the absence of which elitist interests will do the job).

Fragmented Syntax Speaks: Juxtaposition

Amabile structures his opposition to the subject/object-oriented realist symbolic in his first 14-line unit (an intertextual marker and reference to the classical sonnet whose code of 14 lines these lines recall, but whose other codes these lines violate). These lines are fragmented in the first of the ways referred to earlier. The violation of the syntax codes of classical grammar will be obvious here. The overall violation, however, takes the form of a juxtapositional discourse that is older than Homer, and certainly found in Homer. With juxtapositional discourse a "sentence" kernel ("Birdsong" line 1, "Leafless trees" line 5) begins, and the text proceeds in a non-linear way by additive means, which simply add unit upon unit of diegetic (descriptive) semantic meaning as data. This produces in "First Light" the textual effect of a description without a human observer or consciousness doing the observing or describing. This absence of the human observer as subject parallels the absence of a grammatical subject in the syntax fragments. Translated, the fragment "Birdsong" at the beginning would become the syntactically correct "I hear a bird's song," or something like that.

The reference to Homer and juxtapositional discourse above was not accidental. Bruno Snell in *The Discovery of Mind* and Julian Jaynes in *The Origin of Consciousness in the Breakdown of the Bicameral Mind* both write convincingly about the absence of self-consciousness among the archaic Greeks, about the gods speaking through and for those people. (We might say today that fully social discourse codes of a certain kind spoke through them.) With the coming of a money economy, alphabetic writing, philosophy and plain prose discourse, this preconscious gave way to the self-consciousness or early autonomous individualism of the classical Greeks at what many people think of as the beginning of western civilization.

Classical Greek civilization overthrew the juxtapositional discourse and the mythos-based archaic Greek oral symbolic for a realist and basically secular written symbolic in which superpositional linear plain prose discourse replaced the juxtapositional archaic Greek practice. Classical Greek culture became self-conscious and entered history as the emergence of written historical narrative (Herodotus, etc.) which replaced the oral performances of bard-poets.

Superpositional Discourse

In lines 15-32, Amabile shifts from the juxtapositional mode of the first 14 lines to conform to the realist, "correct," linear syntactical forms of sentences. However, he now fragments his sentence units in a different way by allowing his widely varying line lengths to dominate his sentences and syntax. This fragments these otherwise "correct" realist sentences to make syntax serve semantic functions, as we saw with the focat of "morning" above, where the line fragments slowed down the reader to produce end-line multi-levelled semantic results.

Historical Emergence of Consciousness

The first 32 lines shift from the juxtapositional mode of the first 14 lines, to the superpositional mode of the rest. As they do so they simulate and recapitulate through their syntactical differences the original historical birth of consciousness among the classical Greeks (textually superpositional) that came out of an opposition to the archaic Greeks (textually juxtapositional), a process that founded western civilization ("First Light"). This process was to be repeated on a different level in the rebirth of historical consciousness with the Renaissance (another sort of "First Light" and realist symbolic) out of the feudal period. Now we can perhaps more fully understand the importance of those two lines (30-31) and their two opposing sets of relationships between the human subject and nature that we examined earlier:

> that I am a part of Nature [at one with nature, medieval]
> the part that watches [17th-century separation from nature]

Consciousness and Writing

Although it involves unconscious and preconscious levels of the mind, writing as we presently understand it remains for the most part a conscious activity. The perspiration of consciously editing and structuring a text according to some standards (including Amabile's fragmented text) must follow the preconscious inspiration that produced something worth editing in the first place. Readers must be taken into account. In realist discourse (in the sense I have been speaking of it here) this conscious activity produces superpositional sequences of grammatically correct sentences that make up a beginning, middle, and end sequence structure, in which we find the thematization and usually the resolution to a problematic. This constantly repeated linear three-part structure informs masses of books in libraries, and habituation to it socially reproduces the ideological notion in the realist mind that consciousness works in a continuous linear manner. But consciousness does not in fact work like that at all. Consciousness that has been subjected to the codes of realist discourse and put in texts does, but that is a quite different matter. The trouble with the ideology of linear consciousness is that we in fact move in and out of consciousness all the time to punctuate it, but from one moment of consciousness to another we do not, and cannot, remember the gaps in between, or where we have been "in" those gaps. How could we? That would require a self-consciousness of a non-selfconscious state. The realist encoded mind must therefore confront a paradox with "First Light": Amabile's text is "unreal" by the linear coherent and cohesive standards of that realism which claims to capture the real, but its fragmented structure conforms to what we know about an actual consciousness that is punctuated with silences, silences like the end of Amabile's lines, from which we move to different semantic levels and associations. Sounds sort of "real" to me, in a "symbolic" way.

Works Cited

Jaynes, Julian. *The Origin of Consciousness in the Breakdown of the Bicameral Mind*. Toronto: University of Toronto Press, 1976.

Snell, Bruno. *The Discovery of Mind*. Trans. T.G. Rosenmeyer. Cambridge: Harvard University Press, 1953.

Arnason's Irony and Vision

Margaret Sweatman

name them
marsh hawk
marigold
winter
crow
raspberry
willow
elm oak ash
every word a world

every world a gathering of words . . .
(Arnason, *Marsh Burning* 64)

These are the rules of my game: to begin with *Marsh Burning* and try to sketch a map of some of Arnason's work, the sites of departure and play, conflations and matrices, the cloud formations. Trust me. This essay draws on several arbitrary strategies, taking advantage of two questionable rules: one, that a lifetime is progressive and paradigmatic, that we *become* ourselves; secondly, that one text serves as the pretext of the next, biographically. There appear two modalities in Arnason's poetry and his prose, a kind of ironic determinism, and a comic "green" vision. Both sides give rise to parodic and postmodern writing, wonderfully artful and sophisticated.

And so, in the beginning, which in this case is 1980, Arnason wrote *Marsh Burning*. Here is Arnason as bard, his long poem forming itself out of myth and evocation:

> driving through New Brunswick
> the sifting rain steady
> on the windshield of my Chev
> you spoke to me Thor
> saying
>
> *Baldur is dead / slain*
> *Baldur*
> *who was white as the snows on Hecla*
> *Loki is free*
> *Fenrir prowls   just beyond the horizon*
> *somewhere over Fundy*[1] (9)

The poet's voice is an assembly of fragmented voices. This invocatory voice is unusual, even for an adept stylist like Arnason. In *Marsh Burning*, he tunnels through memory, naming, naming: birds, berries, trees, fish, flowers and flies. But freshly named in a heterogeneous, shifty new context. There is an Old Testament quality in this naming, and in the biblical rhythms and inversions: "never have I seen so many rainbows / and so much traffic in the heavens" (12). Warm-blooded rhythms of water and waves: "the liquid harmonics of waves / eroding a shore" (28). And litanies of "accidents," misalliances with fate. In most of Arnason's work, even when

---

1 In Norse mythology, Baldur was the son of sunlight, of life, of innocence and virtue, killed somehow by Loki, a trickster god. And Fenrir, "the son of Loki and an enormous wolf and storm creature, swallowed the sun to bring about Ragnarok, the end of the world" (Lenoski 315).

it's funny, there is a sense of foreboding and profound ambivalence—"*Baldur is dead . . . Loki is free. . . .*" Loki is a trickster god; this is an entropic world, located in the body and in "systems / the neutral distillations of decay . . ." (33):

> all the permutations of despair
> along the axis of event
> death by drowning
> death by traffic accident
> death by gunshot
> death by disease
> death by deception
> death by decay
> death by the slow
> inertial circling of the clock (35)

It will be a long and curious voyage to *The Happiest Man in the World*, his latest collection of stories (1989). While these kinds of psychological speculations about the author are invasive and probably fraudulent, an ancient apprehension surfaces again and again in a kind of urban panic in the later stories, a refrain—"Something is terribly, terribly wrong" ("Economic Crisis" 90).

But *Marsh Burning* begins like an Icelandic saga, "along the axis of event." I know little enough about this form, but my preliminary research has been interesting as it connects with prairie literature and Arnason's distinctive place here. Northrop Frye writes that the saga is a narrative where "the primary interest is in telling the story" (58). Robert Scholes says about the saga:

> As the legend is based on an ideal which serves a real need, the saga is based on a reality, the tie of blood, which has its own ideals: the community of blood, vengeance in blood, the vendetta, marriage, kinship, heritage, patrimony, heredity. Around these concepts the saga gravitates. It is actualized in the Icelandic

> family sagas, in biblical genealogies, in song and story everywhere. It is rooted in the past, in family history and heritage, and its values are as powerful as those of the legend, though less idealistic. (44)

We see this often and variously in Arnason, as in the short story "Sons and Fathers, Fathers and Sons." A community of blood, a blood reality. Something happens to the collection of words that comprise *Marsh Burning*, something happens to "poetry." Consider the assumption that poetry is a special discourse, in Scholes' words, a poetic diction "dominated by the lexical and paradigmatic side of language . . ." (62). What happens when the poet leases out his voice, his "poetic diction," his Special Place? As in *Marsh Burning*, the poem becomes a meeting place for many voices. The poet becomes a ventriloquist. But more on this later; return to the poem.

The names are contextual, evoking a landscape and memory of home. Names are dug out of the sediment; objects sit there, on the page, as momentous and autotelic as William Carlos Williams' wheelbarrow (*Marsh Burning* 84). In a flooded and burning garden, Arnason's marsh, a margin between land and lake:

> white geese rising from a field of summer snow
> leaving it fallow   their crazed crackling
> lingers after they have flown   mad blackbirds
> flash red chevrons crying *kyrie eleison*
> a sloughpump gurgles in a shallow swamp
> overhead sandpipers whimper and wheel
> snipes whistle in their sudden dives
> ducks croak and call   splashing in stagnant
> sloughs smoke hovers on the spare horizon . . .
> (*Marsh Burning* 79)

This passage has some of the characteristics of Anglo-Saxon verse: alliterative lines containing four principal stresses, sometimes divided by a medial caesura, or pause (*Norton*

Anthology 18). Listen to it, that solemn measure and musical phonetics—alliteration seems childlike, imitative, echoic. And "*kyrie eleison*," lord have mercy. The landscape is beautiful, and predatory. There's something magical in this faith that naming makes a world—"say it and make it happen" (*Marsh Burning* 64); and in the formal dignity of the verse, something of ritual and incantation.

There is so much movement in *Marsh Burning*, between the five sections, wave rhythms, especially Section III, which is comprised of sequences repeated and revealed in greater detail, a spatial narrative, an accretion of nouns and gerunds. Section III-1 defines what it isn't: It isn't "strawberries on a bed of clay / poplar roots against an eroding shore . . . ," and it isn't "wet stones at the edge of a lake. / Or even the scent of hay / rotting in a field flooded / by June rains" (39). It isn't these things, the marsh, the sky—there are hawks on these pages, Arnason says so, but that isn't it:

> It is the hold the mind takes
> on these things:
> the green of July   yellow of August
> ochre of a September day.
> Not rain but the slope of rain
> not snow but the curve of drifting fields
> fluttering whiteness of December
> like the unexpected sharpness
> of mint   childhood
> and a fire when it's
> much too late. (39)

It's a poem of sentences. Line breaks accent the elegant prose rhythms, a graceful syntax. "Not rain but the slope of rain / not snow but the curve of drifting fields"—not the particular but the form of the particular, its determinants, a place to start as at the start of a game, submitting to the rules for the pleasure of a singular game, "a pleasure of performance" (Barthes 9).

Marsh Burning is mostly vignettes, or anecdotes.[2] Listen to the brutal stories in Section IV. (Later, we'll hear similar voices telling tender funny tales in "50 Stories and a Piece of Advice.") Death is an unpredictable and violent incident, a moment without moral centre, a private experience. These aren't Arnason's memories; he has spooked up the stories of the place, encounters with Loki, the trickster god. And the stories are told as if naïvely. Arnason borrows a linguistic code which he has—lost, maybe, if that's possible: in this section of *Marsh Burning* and in "50 Stories and a Piece of Advice," he mimics a *restricted* code, switching from an *elaborated* linguistic code. To explain, this, from Mary Douglas, *Natural Symbols*:

> Each type of speech code [restricted, and elaborated] is generated in its own type of social matrix. . . . The restricted code is deeply enmeshed in the immediate social structure, utterances have a double purpose: they convey information, yes, but they also express the social structure, embellish and reinforce it. . . . In its more extreme, elaborate form it is so much disengaged from the normal social structure that it may even come to dominate the latter and require the social group to be structured around the speech, as in the case of a university lecture. (44)

Mary Douglas says that elaborate language, what we might call "highly articulate" language, can determine its own social setting. In *Marsh Burning*, in all of Arnason's work, we see that the linguistic code determines the "story." In Arnason, the stylist, discourse and story are one.

---

2 The *Oxford English Dictionary* definition has figurative resonance:

> *vignette* n. Decorative design, usu. small, on blank space in book, having edges shading off into surrounding paper; photograph with edges shading off into background; (fig.) character sketch or short description.

> *In the end I suppose I don't believe in the notion of the self as some individual generating system pumping these things out. I think of us all as composed of those chunks of discourse, those little observations we or our friends have made at various times. And I think you can pick them up whole hog and use them. I want my readers to be interested, to enjoy these things: they're fragments of other stories, stories caught within stories, anecdotes told inside anecdotes. All the boxes you can open and try and unfold.* (Arnason, "Story Forming" 103)

The sketches in Section IV recall the misshapen moments when time bent for these anonymous speakers. These are the torn edges of poetry, this flat discourse, "low mimesis."[3] The interpolated prose passages refuse to lift, to transform themselves in any fashion:

> I never told this story before. Me and Jerry had gone looking for crayfish along Willow Creek. About a mile west of highway eight where the creek makes that hairpin bend we saw an old lady sitting in the mud by the edge of the water. She had no shoes on, and her face and hair were all covered with blood. She was crying with loud bawling moans, just screaming, there in the middle of nowhere. I guess we should have asked her what was wrong, but we were so scared we just ran home. I guess she must have been o.k. though. I never heard of no old lady dying on Willow Creek. (*Marsh Burning* 59)

---

3 Northrop Frye, *Anatomy of Criticism*:

> If superior neither to other men nor to his environment, the hero is one of us; we respond to a sense of his common humanity, and demand from the poet the same canons of probability that we find in our own experience. This gives us the hero of the low mimetic mode, of most comedy and of realistic fiction. (34)

The deliberate ungrammaticality ("I never heard of no old lady . . .") and an emphatic deictic[4] ("where the creek makes that hairpin bend . . .") gesture toward a world. Until Section IV, *Marsh Burning* has named a natural world; now, Arnason is speaking for a social (economic) context. With the shift of discourse, we experience a perceptual reversal—"*every world a gathering of words*" (64). Style is dominant, style is vision.[5] Diction determines the action or the movement and the narrative rhythm of the piece.

It's beautiful and moving, and there is so much death and hardship in the fifth and final section of *Marsh Burning*, I feel as though I'm reading the darkest prairie realism, different in emphasis from Arnason's later, comic fiction. In this section, Arnason has selected bits of archival material in the form of letters—again, voicings—broken up and interspersed with poetic lines. His technique of merging poetry and document differs in tone from the parodic stylizations of his later work. The voices are appropriated and naturalized in a fairly seamless poetic context. I don't know whether, or to what extent, Arnason has manipulated the archival documents. They are dated 1876 and 1878. Reading them, I enjoy the distance, the defamiliarization, that comes with wandering through a language-museum, that pleasurable perceptual jolt from time-travel. One of the letters, Daniel Lenoski tells us, "is *probably* fictional rather than found." We don't know

4 Jonathan Culler writes:

> Deictics are "orientational" features of language which relate to the situation of utterance, and for our purposes the most interesting are the first and second person pronouns (whose meaning in ordinary discourse is "the speaker" and "the person addressed"), anaphoric articles and demonstratives which refer to an external context rather than to other elements in the discourse, adverbials of place and time whose reference depends on the situation of utterance (here, there, now, yesterday) and verb tenses, especially the non-timeless present. (165)

5 The concept of "style as vision" is explained in Genette 158-59.

the origins of these words. Lenoski is undecided: "Voyaging along postmodern frontiers, the author is *perhaps* trying to blur fiction and history" (Lenoski 317, emphasis mine).

The postmodern strategy of appropriation presents what to my mind is an unresolvable debate, eloquently put forth by Frank Davey in *Reading Canadian Reading*. There isn't room here, thank god, to paraphrase Davey's complex position. In part, Davey says,

> What political relationship is implied when one "speaks for" the interests of another? Whose interests are served? What distinguishes appropriation from expropriation, or exploitation?—representation from misrepresentation? Can there be an act of appropriation, when the oral text is not available as a written text but must be re-invented, re-represented as writing? (225-26)

It seems that some of the anxiety about "the postmodern strategy of appropriation" stems from the belief in an original voice, that is, one that belongs to me and only me and you can't use it and I can't use yours. Davey is too intelligent and sophisticated to argue this, but there is something puritanical about his anxiety, as if literature must be purified of its trespasses. It seems to me (and this isn't a radical position on my part) that literature is always and entirely composed of trespasses, violations, translations from one tongue to another, intertextuality—appropriation.

Davey writes briefly but specifically about some of Arnason's poetry. He overlooks *Marsh Burning*, but focuses for a moment on "Descartes & Dick." We will use this as a junction between *Marsh Burning* and Arnason's subsequent work.

Davey distinguishes those writers who "foreground the constructedness of their representations of voice (often marking them with signs of parody or stylization)" from those who "[use] it [the vernacular, or the strategy of appropriation] from within the aesthetics of realism, as if [they] were able to represent, recreate, the actual discourse of [their] subjects" (223). Stylizations, parody, and meta-narrative (where the writer foregrounds, or makes obvious, the artificiality of this relationship between the writer, the page, and the reader: if I were to say, hi mum, I'm writing an essay now, how'm I doin')—these are several of the favoured techniques of that somewhat mysterious enterprise called postmodernism. Arnason's treatment of document, of the vernacular, in *Marsh Burning* is more in the realist camp. He doesn't disconnect us from our illusion that these people are speaking their *true* tongue. But "Descartes & Dick" lives in a different world. Davey observes that in this later poem Arnason's tactic of "appropriation is focussed not toward 'realizing' the appropriated figure but . . . toward creating a textual/ epistemological structure that dwarfs its representation of any individual figure" (223). The poet takes great delight in artifice. The poem is a construct of sabotage, parody, and pun. The language is something like graffiti: fractured cliché and cartoon, playfully redundant and noisy. The birds "were singing in Latin / I picked out a *Colaptes Auratus* / a *Dendroica Magnolia* and a couple of *Paradidae* . . ." ("Descartes" 64). A flicker, a warbler, and a couple of titmice. The words are so saturated with metalanguage,[6] they resist clear communication, obstruct the traffic on the vertical axis. "I looked for a sign / I couldn't find one anywhere . . ." ("Descartes" 64).

> RENE DESCARTES AND DEADWOOD DICK: A SENTIMENTAL POEM IN SEVERAL CANTOS CONTAINING A THRILLING LOVE STORY, A NARROW ESCAPE FROM HOSTILE INDIANS AND A NUMBER OF PERTINENT PHILOSOPHICAL OBSERVATIONS ALL TOGETHER WITH A GUEST APPEARANCE BY THE AUTHOR HIMSELF. (64)

---

6 A metalanguage talks about either itself or any other language (Lyons 171, 322).

Like a barker at a fair, the poet cajoles his reader, yelling in the library. He disrupts the hallowed, whispery liaison between the reader and his book. The poem has two titles. "Descartes & Dick" is the label of a commodity, a visual hook, and functions as such in Davey's *literary* essay. In contrast, the irreverent verbal description above interjects loudly, flaunting its contents like typographic trinkets on the silent page.[7]

Davey's is a rich observation about "Descartes & Dick": a "structure that dwarfs its representation of any individual figure." (There are a lot of dwarfs in Arnason's *oeuvre*, but that's beside the point.) As structure is foregrounded, the "individual figure" or character recedes in importance and becomes a ripple on the surface of the text, a "function" of the narrative.[8]

Arnason tells us:

> *I'm interested particularly in solving narrative problems. How you can tell a story that has certain restraints, certain limitations. Then I start to write and whatever story comes, comes. So, the ideas for the stories come after the form for the stories. The idea is secondary—it doesn't matter what it's about. I have no idea what story it's going to be when I start and I have no idea where it's going to go. As a matter of fact, perhaps a slight confession, one of my principles of composition is to eliminate possible endings. If I'm writing and I think of a neat way of ending the story then I*

7 On the subject of titles in a print culture, see Walter Ong 125-26.

8 "Function" is defined by Robert Scholes in his appraisal of the accomplishments of the Russian formalist Vladimir Propp. Scholes writes, "Propp arrives at the principle that though the personages of a [folk]tale are variable, their functions in the tales are constant and limited." Some "personages" of the folktale, named by Propp, are the hero, the false hero, the villain, the victim. Function is "an act of a character, defined from the point of view of its significance for the course of the action . . ." (Scholes 63).

> *automatically exclude it. I'm a real believer in the process of writing.* ("Story Forming" 101)

Form. Let's start with a story from *50 Stories and a Piece of Advice* (1982). Take "The Sunfish." Here's a story that plays (*plays*: an operative word in Arnason's technique) with the Icelandic family saga. The "main character," Gusti Oddson, is an odd old man to whom the narrator claims kin:

> Dawn was just spreading its red glow across Lake Winnipeg when Gusti Oddson reached for the buoy to pull in the first of his seven nets. And what was he thinking, that second cousin once removed of my great-grandmother, on a June morning in 1878? Perhaps he was thinking of the smallpox epidemic that had recently taken his wife and three children, or perhaps he was thinking about nets and why they sometimes caught fish and sometimes didn't. He wasn't thinking about talking fish, or at least the scattered diaries he left behind him give no indication that he was thinking about talking fish, and why, after all, should he have been? That's why he was startled when the sunfish he had just pulled into his boat, the first sunfish of the day, spoke to him. (61)

The first sentence is deceptively conventional, inviting our indulgence in a fiction. The story-teller's traditional method of introducing information on the heels of the action, that seems conventional too. But the rhythm of this paragraph swings, "And what was he thinking . . . Perhaps he was thinking . . . perhaps he was thinking . . . He wasn't thinking . . . That's why he was startled. . . ." Repetitive, subjunctive. The entire story is dominated by the game of the subjunctive, and dominated by rhythm, as Gusti the fisherman is dominated by the wish granted by the sunfish. Gusti is a function of the course of action, the inevitable wish. And again, the gesture toward a documented context, the diaries, the shameless avowal of Truth.

This story is knit with bright, folk-art materials. Gusti's shack, which he cleans "inside and out, including the roof" (66) to the amazement of the community: "The entire community came out to watch him with wonder" (66). It's a fishing village, a settlement community, a tribe, full of song and wonder, flirtations, in the sway of a moral code both puritanical and permissive, scandalous and scandalized. Blankets of the finest wool (yes sir yes sir), a brick chimney, the garden behind the house, poppies blooming in primary colours, blue-eyed golden-haired Freya.

> The ox stopped right at the foot of the dock, and Freya climbed into the wagon and seated herself in the lap of the god. She began the oration, and all the community sat down on the ground to listen. . . . She spoke of rain. She spoke of sunlight and crops. She spoke of trees bursting out of the earth, of animals in the fields, of nets dripping with fish. She spoke of love and of little children. Her voice mingled with the voices of birds and the lapping of waves. And then she was gone. (72)

"She began . . . She spoke . . . She spoke . . . She spoke . . . She spoke . . . Her voice . . . And then. . . ." Repetition, rhythm, harmony, organic unity, fertility: the comic vision. There follows a communal feast, a temporary truce in the social contract. Love and springtime are in ascendency. But look at this, what is this fresh arrangement: a new-fangled agreement between writer and reader. The joy conveyed by these stories is thematic, yes, but more: something has happened to the words. It's as if the writer is playing on those fine fibres between the words and their referents, *playing* the joyfully arbitrary connections between signifier and signified.

There are semantic ramifications too, of course. "The Sunfish" is open-ended. The story-teller breaks through the surface, toward the end of the tale, in the midst of Gusti's affirmative homiletic on the subject of love. "Here you must bear with me," says the narrator (74). You and me: the love poem. The direct address reveals the reading/writing process—and as it does, many things shift: it demystifies the Author; we find out Oz is a bag o' wind manipulated by a shy but compassionate guy backstage. "The Sunfish" has multiple and provisional endings offered to us with a good-natured humility that is thoroughly stylistic, a posture. The story is resistant to the very possibility of a monological theory of origin.

We learn that this is "postmodernism," and go to Northrop Frye and Linda Hutcheon for advice. Linda Hutcheon tells us that postmodern art

> asserts and deliberately undermines such principles as value, order, meaning, control, and identity . . . that have been the basic premises of bourgeois liberalism. Those humanistic principles are still operative in our culture, but for many they are no longer seen as eternal and unchallengeable. . . . Such a process reveals rather than conceals the tracks of the signifying systems that constitute our world—that is, systems constructed by us in answer to our needs. However important these systems are, they are not natural, given, or universal. (13)

It's illuminating to read Hutcheon on postmodernism in tandem with Bakhtin, Frye, and others, on the carnivalesque, Menippean satire, and comedy. Ideas reappear in various ways. Time and again, I am reminded of Arnason's stratagem. Menippean satire and the carnivalesque are companionable, especially as they have been imported to our locale. Frye writes:

> The Menippean satire deals less with people as such than with mental attitudes. Pedants, bigots, cranks, parvenus, virtuosi, enthusiasts, rapacious and incompetent professional men of all kinds, are handled in terms of their occupational approach to life as distinct from their social behavior. The Menippean satire thus resembles the confession in its ability to handle

> abstract ideas and theories, and differs from the novel in its characterization, which is stylized rather than naturalistic.... The novelist sees evil and folly as social diseases, but the Menippean satirist sees them as diseases of the intellect.... (309)

Many of Arnason's short stories are written as first-person narratives in the "confessional" voice of a professional modern man offering his rather callow observations. We see this in "The Marriage Inspector," "My Baby and Me" (though this narrator sings such a rhythmic tale full of love and optimism), "Sons and Fathers, Fathers and Sons," "The Figure Skater," "Mary Yvette," "Falling in Love with Alice," "The Drunk Woman Is Singing in My Office" (all from *The Circus Performers' Bar*), and "The Happiest Man in the World."

In many stories too, the narrative is attenuated in favour of a satiric demography, comprised of a series of not-so-companionable raids on the "occupational approach to life": "The Boys," "All the Elements," "The Artist," "The Professor" (all from *The Circus Performers' Bar*). In "The Professor," generic professors, wives, graduate students, and "little long-legged girls" (95) serve as indices in a census; the "characters' " agency diminished, the "action" subsumed under generalizing iterations.[9] But for all its satiric diminishment, this story closes with a verbal mediation, a cosmic ambivalence which I think is thoroughly rhetorical, and characteristic of Arnason's stylistic ironies:

> They know nothing, those brown girls, though their lilting voices ripple through the sad, betrayed hallways. They think they will live forever. The professor in his

---

9 Gerard Genette, *Narrative Discourse*:

> This type of narrative, where a single narrative utterance takes upon itself several occurrences together of the same event (in other words, once again, several events considered only in terms of their analogy), we will call iterative narrative. (116)

> book-lined office reads the desire in their flowing scripts. He prays for them. May they be happy. May they live long. May the loving gods release them into flowering fields, blue waters and the sun's enduring light. (98)

Mikhail Bakhtin relates Menippean satire both to the serio-comical and carnivalesque folklore. Of the genres of the serio-comical, Bakhtin writes,

> In all genres of the serio-comical, to be sure, there is a strong rhetorical element, but in the atmosphere of *joyful relativity* characteristic of a carnival sense of the world this element is fundamentally changed: there is weakening of its one-sided rhetorical seriousness, its rationality, its singular meaning, its dogmatism. (107)

Bakhtin goes on (and on) to say that the serio-comical genres are multi-styled and multi-voiced, making use of various authorial masks. "Alongside the representing word there appears the represented word: in certain genres a leading role is played by the double-voiced word" (108). This sounds a lot like the stylizations and parody that Linda Hutcheon describes in her definitions of postmodernism: the role of duplicity in postmodern narratives.[10] I'm pressing the limits of my space here, but one more observation seems necessary. Bakhtin writes that in the Menippea:

---

10 See Hutcheon 39-42. In part, Hutcheon argues:

> Many of the foes of postmodernism see irony as fundamentally anti-serious, but this is to mistake and misconstrue the critical power of double-voicing. As Umberto Eco has said, about both his own historiographic metafiction and his semiotic theorizing, the "game of irony" is intricately involved in seriousness of purpose and theme. In fact irony may be the only way we *can* be serious today. There is no innocence in our world, he suggests. We cannot ignore the discourses that precede and contextualize everything we say and do, and it is through ironic parody that we signal our awareness of this inescapable fact. The "already-said" must be reconsidered and can be reconsidered only in an ironic way. . . . (39)

> Dreams, daydreams, insanity destroy the epic and tragic wholeness of a person and his fate: the possibilities of another person and another life are revealed in him, he loses his finalized quality and ceases to mean only one thing; he ceases to coincide with himself. . . . This destruction of the wholeness and finalized quality of a man is facilitated by the appearance, in the menippea, of a dialogic relationship to one's own self (fraught with the possibility of split personality). (116-17)

"I am not myself today" (*Marsh Burning* 80). Characters, and the narrators too, are not synchronous with their circumstances. Their "being" is delayed by the intellect. We find speakers on an endless quest for "something else," some hapless adultery. In a skilful and funny story called "Do Astronauts Have Sex Fantasies?" which is composed entirely of random questions, the "narrator" asks,

> Who actually buys books of poetry and reads them? What happens to all the paintings of failed artists when they die? Why do you keep smoking when you know what it is doing to your lungs? Why can't you resist that extra glass of wine with supper, that extra glass of brandy after dessert, when you know what it is doing to your liver? Why are you so filled with lust and yearning and desire? Why does your weakness threaten to overwhelm everything you do? Doesn't anybody care? (94)

Because the narratives put so many rhetorical determinants into play, the Arnason stories become vastly different from realist fiction. These stories have been processed, programmed, coded, in a way that realist fiction pretends not to be. Even a comparatively conventional story like "The Happiest Man in the World" has this deliberately stylized quality. It *foregrounds its own constructedness*, as words are repeated and recontextualized until they become musical, "represented words." Sentences are simple, rarely fused, and they have an up-and-down cadence, a kind of 4\4 rhythm which suggests an innocent, guileless narrator. We see ourselves in our posturings and needs, ourselves as anxious but eager consumers, yearning for individuality. We would love to be "characters." The story-teller forgives us, releases us, into our delightful errors:

> Sharon wanted to know what the story meant, but I told her that it was just a story and it didn't mean anything. A warm breeze had sprung up as we walked, and small waves splashed at our feet. A full moon glinted yellow off the lake. We rolled up our jeans and walked in the little waves all the way back to the cottage. Then we took off all our clothes and went skinny dipping. We decided that a little later we would make love. (142)

Arnason's professional characters *decide* to make love: pure impulses and desires, quantified and coded. His stories reject monological meaning and referentiality; "it was just a story and it didn't mean anything." Elsewhere, Arnason has said, "I wasn't telling a truth, I was making a thing" ("Story Forming" 102). Such a claim for autonomy is at odds, or perhaps better, complements, my observation that Arnason's characters are demographic, coded, ciphers.

As I said earlier, there are a lot of dwarfs in these pages. In "Story Forming," Arnason says that in his opinion, "we're all discrete grotesques in one way or another" (105). We read in "The Circus Performers' Bar": "Here I sit, burning with love, aching with desire, stunted, dwarfed, and out in the street, already, the guns are beginning" (142). In "The Girl of Milk and Blood":

> See us for what we were, what we are. Our bodies stunted and deformed, half men always on the look-out for the kick, the beating that the others must give because we affront them by wrapping desire in such awkward flesh. We are comic at a distance, terrifying when we're near, conjuring in every man the dwarf within. (154)

Both stories (and "The Committee" from *The Circus Performers' Bar* as well) are recontextualizations of Snow White and the Seven Dwarfs. The speaker, therefore, is a dwarf: the word *dwarf*, preceding quotation marks.

This a paradox: In "Story Forming," Arnason says, "I'm interested in fairy tales because it seems to me there are truths in them other than those which appear on the surface" (107). And in "The Girl of Milk and Blood," one of the narrators (a dwarf) observes, "After a while, you know them all, all the languages. They say the same things in the same rhythms so that you learn that meaning is not in the words but in the patterns, some grammar common to them all for which the words are merely clothing" (147-48). Surface appearance, rhythm, repetition, system or pattern conceal deeper level truths which are sometimes allowed to emerge and which sometimes emerge by themselves.

Earlier I quoted part of a statement by Robert Scholes. Here it is again, enlarged:

> In poetry the lexical and paradigmatic side of language dominates—the reverberations of a given word in its own linguistic heritage. Naturally, this is, as Robert Frost said, "what gets lost in translation." Poetry celebrates the unique in a culture, a language, a man's way of using his language. In myth, however, the structural and syntagmatic side of language dominates, and at this level languages have much in common. Linguistic structure, and hence myths, have a universality which linguistic units, being arbitrary, do not have. (62)

For myth, we can substitute fairy tale. And for fairy tale, we can substitute stories dominated by rhythm and repetition, and structure. But I find this strange. The same writer who resists closure, who emphasizes surface play, who opens the narrator and the fictional character to notions of dialogism and discourse, also appeals to a universal structure that yields, maybe not Truth, but at least meaning which might enjoy some freedom from context, in an appeal to universality.

That's not it. By shifting the emphasis to structure and the syntagmatic axis[11] we become aware of the hitherto hidden processes of meaning-making. In Arnason's wilful fictions, especially these fairy tales, the language is so obviously artificial, his regular syntax given such a comical foreign accent, we become aware that the fabrication and the discourse determine meaning. And the act of mythography becomes visible:

> I should have gone to the performance of the Boukevenian dancers at the Palace of the Arts. Afterwards, I might have joined them for supper, plied some savage mountain girl with vodka and wit, and taken her back to my room. We could have made love intensely; I am not an acrobat for nothing. ("Circus" 138)

> *I'm interested in the comic vision. Quite clearly, the last thing I would be remotely interested in writing is a great tragedy. In fact, as far as I can understand it, tragedy, and the ability to respond to tragedy, is essentially a narrow, elitist sensibility of the upper classes that allows them to feel superior to the people in the pit. I'll cast my lot with the people in the pit.* ("Story Forming" 109)

Frye tells us that comedy "usually moves toward a happy ending, and the normal response of the audience to a happy ending is 'this should be,' which sounds like a moral

---

11 Scholes:

> The syntagmatic element of language has to do with the positioning of a sign in any particular utterance. In a given sentence, for example, the meaning of a single word is determined partly by its position in the sentence and its relation to the other words and grammatical units of that sentence. This is the word's syntagmatic (linear, diachronic) aspect, often conceptualized as a horizontal axis along which the sentence is spread out in its necessary order. (18-19)

judgement. So it is, except that it is not moral in the restricted sense, but social" (167). Arnason's gentle ambivalent satires often conclude on the social level:

> This is where the story ends, at the moment of the kiss. It goes on and on forever while cities burn, nations rise and fall, galaxies are born and die, and the universe snuffs out the stars one by one. It goes on, the story, the brush of a kiss. ("Girl's Story" 130)

These stories leave us in an entropic green world: Loki remains at large, with the victory of love and a sense of rebirth, all as part of a fictional structure, open-ended or circular. It ends here, within the boundaries of the fictional patterns, the play of patterns on the page. We "Square Dancers" dance in a textual world:

> Only this much is known. Somewhere, outside, people are dying in El Salvador and Chile, the stockpile of bombs is rising, the lakes are dying and the sea is out of control. Inside, they bow to their partners, they take their places in the square, and when the caller's voice begins its old familiar cry, they dance, never missing a beat. ("Square Dancers" 81)

Works Cited

Arnason, David. *The Circus Performers' Bar*. Vancouver: Talonbooks, 1984.

__________. "The Circus Performers' Bar." *The Circus Performers' Bar* 137-42.

__________. "Descartes & Dick." *Skrag*. Winnipeg: Turnstone Press, 1987. 63-71.

__________. "Do Astronauts Have Sex Fantasies?" *The Circus Performers' Bar* 91-94.

__________. "The Economic Crisis." *The Circus Performers' Bar* 87-90.

_________. *50 Stories and a Piece of Advice*. Winnipeg: Turnstone Press, 1982.

_________. "50 Stories and a Piece of Advice." *50 Stories and a Piece of Advice* 1-16.

_________. "The Girl of Milk and Blood." *The Circus Performers' Bar* 143-57.

_________. "A Girl's Story." *The Circus Performers' Bar* 123-30.

_________. *The Happiest Man in the World*. Vancouver: Talonbooks, 1989.

_________. "The Happiest Man in the World." *The Happiest Man in the World* 136-42.

_________. *Marsh Burning*. Winnipeg: Turnstone Press, 1980. Rpt. in *a/long prairie lines: An Anthology of Long Prairie Poems*. Ed. Daniel S. Lenoski. Winnipeg: Turnstone Press, 1989. 257-317.

_________. "The Professor." *The Circus Performers' Bar* 95-98.

_________. "Sons and Fathers, Fathers and Sons." *The Circus Performers' Bar* 37-48.

_________. "Square Dancers." *The Circus Performers' Bar* 79-81.

_________. "Story Forming." *Trace: Prairie Writers on Writing*. Ed. Birk Sproxton. Winnipeg: Turnstone Press, 1986. 101-09.

_________. "The Sunfish." *50 Stories and a Piece of Advice* 61-75.

Bakhtin, Mikhail. *Problems of Dostoevsky's Poetics*. Ed. and trans. Caryl Emerson. Minneapolis: University of Minnesota Press, 1984, 1987.

Barthes, Roland. *The Pleasure of the Text*. Trans. Richard Miller. New York: The Noonday Press; Farrar, Straus and Giroux, 1975, 1989.

Culler, Jonathan. *Structuralist Poetics: Structuralism, Linguistics and the Study of Literature*. London: Routledge and Kegan Paul, 1975, 1983.

Davey, Frank. "A Young Boy's Eden: Notes on Recent 'Prairie' Poetry." *Reading Canadian Reading*. Winnipeg: Turnstone Press, 1988. 213-29.

Douglas, Mary. *Natural Symbols: Explorations in Cosmology*. London: Penguin, 1978.

Frye, Northrop. *Anatomy of Criticism: Four Essays*. Princeton: Princeton University Press, 1957, 1967.

Genette, Gerard. *Narrative Discourse: An Essay in Method*. Trans. Jane E. Lewin. Ithaca: Cornell University Press, 1980, 1987.

Hutcheon, Linda. *A Poetics of Postmodernism: History, Theory, Fiction*. New York: Routledge, 1988.

Lenoski, Daniel S., ed. *a/long prairie lines: An Anthology of Long Prairie Poems*. Winnipeg: Turnstone Press, 1989.

Lyons, John. *Language and Linguistics: An Introduction*. Cambridge: Cambridge University Press, 1981, 1984.

The Norton Anthology of English Literature. 3rd ed. Description of Old and Middle English Prosody. New York: W.W. Norton & Company, 1975.

Ong, Walter. *Orality and Literacy*. London: Methuen, 1982.

Oxford English Dictionary. 1978.

Scholes, Robert. *Structuralism in Literature: An Introduction*. New Haven: Yale University Press, 1974, 1976.

13 Ways of Looking at Pat Friesen

Wayne Tefs

1. Child of Adamantine Soil

Steinbach, Manitoba is a town of some 5000 located 35 miles south and east of Winnipeg, just outside the fertile Red River plain and in the heart of the province's Anabaptist community. A commercially progressive town which has systematically resisted the encroachment of trade unions into its business enterprises and rejected such modern demons as beer parlours and movie theatres, it boasts an up-to-date hockey arena, a dozen automobile dealerships and as many churches, notably absent among these the Roman Catholic. On first contact a clean, quiet place, streets swept, storefronts freshly painted, citizens briskly going about their business. A place to raise children far from the press of polyglot, techno-pop metropoli celebrated in glossy magazines and slick films. To some residents it is more familiarly known as "Stony Creek"—a name that reflects the town's Germanic roots as well as its adamantine soil.

Patrick Friesen knows that soil well. Steinbach and its environs are his home turf. His family has lived in the area for several generations. He was born there, went to school there, and cruised Main Street in a '59 Chevy as a teenager—I was there, too—and later, gravel back roads with a box of beer. Sowed the first seeds of love there. Left there when teachers, church elders and family proved too resistant a plot for a wild-eyed, young thinker of the sixties. Friesen is Steinbach's first poet, and he understands how that stony land shrivels the souls of those planted in its uncompromising soil:

> lean and stark apart,
> striding across the stubbled earth,
> the old man knew the hairs of sorrow.
> each knuckle of his hands a fist,
> each finger a bent direction.
>
> (he knew the plod of a slow horse
> with dust like chaff at its feet,
> the Sunday chat of hens
> making a stillness in the barn.)
>
> and he knew the clatter of clay
> on a box, where his woman lay.
>
> his mouth a wound,
> his voice harsh
> and his words graceless,
> he sat gaunt in his straight chair,
> unlamenting. (*lands* 12)

2. Student of Spiritual Quests

"Stark," "bent," "plod," "wound." Words that suggest one aspect of growing up in an authoritarian environment. They occur often in Friesen's poetry. The essential experiences of Mennonite upbringing as he renders them are alienating. He speaks of the need to escape this background in a favourite phrase, "self exile." Another favourite is "stone," often counterpointed imagistically and thematically with "garden." They reflect Friesen's landscape: the country around Steinbach is unyielding, it resists gardens. But these images also reflect the poet's mind, struggling to locate a paradise in the resistant soil of Mennonitism. So landscape transforms into mindscape. In the poem above, the images close on the telling abstractions, "graceless" and "unlamenting." Do these words depict the definitive small-town Mennonite experience in the Cold War era? Perhaps not. But neither do they paint a pretty portrait of the place that made the speaker. Not the sort of soil we expect to nurture a poet.

3. Devotee of the White Aboriginal

Where did the poet come from, then? Clearly not an easy question to answer, given the variety of experiences available to a young intellectual in the sixties and the experimental temper of those times. University friends and the academically inclined would cite the influence of Traherne/Herbert/Donne, the modernist poets, a class in Shakespeare with Vic Cowie, cinema vérité, Russian history. Roommates from Stradbrook Street would counter with John Lennon, *One Flew Over the Cuckoo's Nest*, the Beat poets, Carlos Castenada, love-ins for peace, Woodstock, Bob Dylan. Marijuana. The formula might also include John Berryman, poet obsessed by religious commitment—and thoughts of self-destruction. From these multiple influences flow Friesen's themes. His rhythms and syntax spring from the ritualized litany of the church and its linguistic forging together of worldly authority and other-worldly fervour.

My own memories are of smoke-scarved discussions at the Cambridge Hotel, before the softball teams moved in, before gentrification. The sixties. Country music, stacking chairs, old men with slick shaved faces. Thursday nights over draught and congealing fries. Subject: the works of D.H. Lawrence. What drew Pat Friesen to Lawrence, he claimed, was the visionary novelist's passionate denunciation of mind-centred consciousness, embodied, the argument went, in the characters of Gerald Critchley and Clifford Chatterly. Friesen was fascinated by the metaphysics of primitivism. The rebellious young poet devoured the infamous novelist. They shared aspects of background—proletarian, evangelical—and a determination to leave a mark on the world despite humble origins.

There was, too, a shared fascination with dying and death, although this might not have been acknowledged in Friesen's formative years. And a fervid wrestling, sometimes desperate, always intense, with the roles of men and women in modern love. (Later this fascination would curve, not surprisingly, toward Henry Miller.) Blood consciousness, the moon, shadowy urges and dim passages. The ghosts of Lawrence's "dark gods" whisper through Friesen's poetic lines, as do censures from those who don't share his vision and zealous commitment to the primitive.

4. Image-Forger

From the cover of Friesen's second book of poems, *bluebottle*, stares the poet's photograph, the exposure reversed so that the light and shadow have exchanged their standard places. Friesen's eyes are opaque. Iridescence plays on the margin of his features, expressively shaved by the book's designer, and (for believers) dangerously suggestive of the crucified Christ. The volume was published in 1978 when Friesen was 32. In his twenties he smoked Pall Malls in the film noir manner and wore his hair long, almost hippie style. When, as undergraduates, we experimented with the hirsute, he never was able to mount a satisfactory beard. Now that he's 40 he wears his hair short and brushed back, the same style as his dead father's. Wistful hunger for the past—or fashionable political statement?

5. Son

Poets, W.B. Yeats once said, would die of loneliness but for women, and they choose their men friends so they may have someone to talk about women with. Latter-day romantic that he is, Patrick Friesen's main subject has been a primal relation, too. But the relation that compels him is familial rather than connubial. Friesen's subject is his unresolved relation with the father.

> when you see a man vanishing before you
> your father   the pain in his eyes
> clears and there is no love nor sorrow   the eyes break
> looking   as ma said   toward eternity
> then you know the question and admiration
> are all you have (*Unearthly* 16)

These are the concluding lines from the second poem in a suite entitled the "pa poems" which Friesen placed in his fourth book, *Unearthly Horses*. They register an acute sense of loss which the poet has voiced publicly since the death of his father some 20 years ago, an event which deepens his loss of faith and which dovetails with his assumption of the role of poet. Throughout his writing Friesen has harnessed tone, imagery and form to express this absence, charting as he does in the above lines the gaps, the spaces between his tortured consciousness of the flesh's betrayal and the pains of premature loss. *bluebottle* contains a moving lyric, "closet," which typifies Friesen's fusion of simple utterance with profound insight.

6. Student of Death

> I finger the khaki shirt
> he wore on his last working day
> before he unbuttoned

along the collar   stain of sweat
faint salt smell of him alive
even as he lies
past mattering in the grave

work pants sharply creased
have fallen from the wooden hanger
I see wrinkles behind the knees
where he stooped or bent

lenses of the eye-glasses
reveal striations
of his eye-lashes on dust

I can't imagine what he saw
as he lay thin and bare
in that dark place (*bluebottle* 7)

7. Performer

There is grief here, acute and moving, as there is in any number of Friesen's poems on this subject, from his first book, *the lands i am*, to the recent *Flicker and Hawk*. He has rung the changes on this theme, performed the scales from pain to indignation to rage to guilt and then back to pain again. The pain is authentic. Its evocation is always moving, often haunting in its directness, clarity and candour. Some of these poems are breathtaking, and most memorable. Writing poems of personal loss has often taken courage, but Friesen's obsession with this theme has at times become indulgence, a fact which he acknowledges humorously in "pa poem 8: crying wolf."

listen to this guy crying wolf
kvetching about his old man   pa he calls him
. . . .
just listen to his sickness and self-loathing   moaning
like he's somehow special   as if no one's lost a father
    before (*Unearthly* 24)

8. The Man Who Fell from Grace

Guilt then. And guilt about guilt. If this sounds circular, somewhat confused, it's because the brand of Christianity Friesen grew up with is built on those paradoxes and because sometimes his poetry traces an infinite regression, spiralling back toward some unstated but all-embracing source. The movement begins in personal narrative, what it means to live in a close family, to defy a father, to reject a mother. It loops back to a cultural paradigm where the focus is on fathers and sons, that troubled relation at the centre of Judeo-Christian thinking from the Fall, through Abram and Isaac, to Jesus of Nazareth on the cross uttering his plea for all mankind.

Friesen is, after all, a fallen Mennonite, a man who has turned his back on the Anabaptist community, not so much defying as simply rejecting it as irrelevant to his concerns, and to the concerns of modern man in general. In other words, the rebel. And the rebel has a price to pay. For Friesen it has been the painful knowledge that he has betrayed his past and his culture, the history of his father and his father before him. Not wholly and too stridently. Elegiacally, most often, meditatively, rather. But betrayed none the less. And publicly, in print—and hence in subtle but undeniable opposition to the one true book in his tradition, the Bible.

9. The Conscience of His Race

The weight of that burden on Friesen's back is evident throughout his work, most notably in *The Shunning*, a play whose dramatization of the struggle between authoritarian community and sceptical individual projects Friesen's own deepest anxieties about his place in his society. Perhaps surprisingly, the play was a considerable success when it toured the Mennonite towns of rural Manitoba, the ostensible objects of its criticism. In the play the protagonist stands up to community elders despite the fact that this means exclusion from the society that has nurtured him into manhood.

He is ostracized, in some respects of his own choosing. The play is tortured. It reeks agony, guilt and despair. There is little more than muted joy here, as there is little in Friesen's work as a whole. On closer examination it appears the subtext of this striking play is the poet's anxiety about betraying his fathers—personal and communal. His own words say it best: "Perhaps in standing up for the individual against the attempts of society to stifle his spiritual growth, I might be perceived as a betrayer" ("Poetry" 11).

10. The Long-Legged Fly

Seen from another perspective, and without minimizing the deep personal agony they enact, Friesen's elegiac effusions on the death of his familial father act as agents of expiation. Through them the poet exorcizes the guilt he feels about betraying his social family, his community—a necessary, ongoing betrayal, which is nevertheless profoundly painful, given the communal proscriptions of rural Mennonite society. Hence,

> I can't speak for the others
> almost don't have the heart to speak for myself
> think of me as lost   living
> with one foot in the shade
> trying to be true and double-crossing you every step of
>   the way
> it's something to live with (*Unearthly* 21)

11. Mennonite Manqué

Having abandoned the community of evangelical believers, Friesen embraces the white aboriginal, D.H. Lawrence, dark priest of modern primitivism, a seer who was also a rebel and an outcast. Words such as "instinctive," "dynamic" and "innocence" flash through Friesen's pronouncements on art, culture, society and education. He is drawn to metaphysics and distrusts materialism—Darwin,

Freud, Marx. There is more than a little of the wild-eyed romantic in Friesen's work. His poems champion ritual, gypsy dancing, spontaneous singing, orgiastic sex, and prophets willing to speak in tongues even at the risk of death.

12. Student of Love

He has moments of satori, he says self-mockingly. And he writes not only of the dark, desperate search for meaning, so typical of his Mennonite forebears. There is also the joy of baseball, memories of his mother playing the "Moonlight Sonata" on the piano, twisting, picnics with friends, laughter, puns, memories of Ryan and Ralph and Ed, beer bottles flung from car windows, autumn leaves, Dennis Hopper, lovers, secret teenage moments with Chuck Berry, rye and coke, the limbo, babies' skin. Ecstasy.

13. The Mennonite in Spite of Himself

The centre of Mennonite experience is the truth of the living God. It is manifest in Mennonite devotion, and in the Mennonite quest for wholeness in both this earthly experience and some other life's more sufficient paradise. It is no real surprise to find these elements in abundance in Friesen's poetry. Nor is it surprising to find that two of his consistent motifs are the "garden," on the one hand, and on the other, the "New Jerusalem." One represents the wholeness sought in Christian experience, the other a symbol of its potential in the here-and-now. Like William Blake, Friesen calls the latter "beulah," and writes in one poem:

> I'm singing 'beulah land'   I'm singing elijah
> because I see ahead where I shed my clothes
> maybe hang them in a closet
> and disappear (*Unearthly* 21)

So Friesen joins his Christian ancestors' wilderness trek between the garden and the desert, between the golden age and the millenium. The locus of his spiritual quest is, of course, radically different than his forebears'. Eclectic, secular and carnal. Yet Friesen finds himself alongside them in some important respects, searching in a divided world for spiritual values to make men whole again. Driven even, toward what he calls truth. "I am impatient for that loss," a Christian poet of our century writes, "by which the spirit gains." Pat Friesen might embrace that sentiment, asserting as it does the regeneration of goodness out of the intractable negatives of broken contemporary experience.

Works Cited

Friesen, Patrick. *bluebottle*. Winnipeg: Turnstone Press, 1978.
__________. *Flicker and Hawk*. Winnipeg: Turnstone Press, 1987.
__________. *the lands i am*. Winnipeg: Turnstone Press, 1976.
__________. "The Poetry of Experience." *Prairie Fire* VII.1 (Spring 1986): 5-14.
__________. *The Shunning*. Winnipeg: Turnstone Press, 1980.
__________. *The Shunning*, the play. *New Works*. Toronto: Playwrights Union of Canada, 1987.
__________. *Unearthly Horses*. Winnipeg: Turnstone Press, 1984.

"Drawing /in": Wholeness and Dislocation in the Work of Kristjana Gunnars

Judith Owens

The work of Icelandic-born Kristjana Gunnars, a landed immigrant in Canada since 1969, has earned her increasing recognition as a major Canadian writer. In responding to Gunnars' work—to date, six volumes of poetry, a collection of stories, a novel, and various translations and editions—critics and reviewers have attended, generally, to her treatment of alienation, loss, estrangement, themes very often developed from the perspective of an immigrant, a "hybrid," to use one of Gunnars' own images (*Night Workers* 53), belonging wholly to neither one world nor another. Recently, Paul Hjartarson has identified as most central to Gunnars' writing her exploration of "the loss of a way of life, a world, and with it, of one's identity" (123). In the present essay, I wish to focus not only on the ways in which dislocation, loss, and estrangement inform Gunnars' work, but also on the ways in which these themes take shape against an insistent and pervasive pull towards a vision of wholeness, containment, and community. I will concentrate particularly on Gunnars' fifth volume of poetry, *The Night Workers of Ragnarök*, on both the poems and the author's introduction to the volume, a piece of prose which provides for us far more than mere exposition of the poetry.

i

The title poem and epigraph of the poetic cycle "The Silent Hand" from Gunnars' *The Night Workers of Ragnarök* grows out of, and reflects, a number of Gunnars' characteristic poetic concerns, both formal and thematic. The poem, which I will quote in its entirety, offers an unassumingly quiet gnomic truth:

> we cannot be sure where
> we come from. all
> that matters is
>
> where we long to go
> the silent hand that draws us
> in (73)

Within the immediate context of the poetic cycle, and within the larger context of Gunnars' work, this seemingly simple maxim yields a number of ambivalences, holds in suspension a number of tensions. To begin with, the poem marks a dislocation, a loss of origins and certainty: "we cannot be sure where / we come from." Structurally, too, the poem reflects displacement, the break between the first three and last three lines suggesting the separation of origins and destiny. More than that, the break figures a kind of estrangement: distanced from her origins, the poet has not yet moved into the body of her desire. For a brief moment, the poem holds out the possibility that the hiatus between "where we come from" and "where we long to go" represents stasis or equilibrium. Syntactically, we can read the clause "all / that matters is" as independent, as a statement of fulfilment, of fully realized presence. When we continue reading, however, we recognize that the last three lines complete the sentence beginning in line two with "all." Accordingly, we recognize the moment of stasis as an illusory moment of fulfilment, making even more poignant the poet's sense that her world has not yet assumed the shape of her desire.

Against these indices of dislocation, estrangement, and uncertainty, the poem sketches a very strong pull towards containment, community, and definition. The poet speaks of "the silent hand that draws us / in." She thus implies that to be drawn, in the sense of defined or pictured, means to be drawn into something, and that to be drawn in the sense of guided means similarly to be drawn into something, into a centre, into a circle. The line break enforces these various senses, compelling the recognition that to be defined, or to have one's way defined, involves being sheltered and protected. The poem suggests, too, the complicity of desire in this drawing of containment, for the silent hand draws us to "where we long to go." More particularly, we sense the poet's complicity in this: the writer's hand draws, defines, and leads.

To look at the poem within its immediate context, the poetic cycle entitled "The Silent Hand," allows us to see the poet's hand at work, trying to draw together vastly different worlds and as well trying to pull together parts of what she feels to be a divided self.

The cycle, occasioned by one of Gunnars' return visits to her native Iceland, deals with the whaling industry of that country. In the Introduction to the volume, Gunnars says that in this sequence she "made an effort to reconcile [her] sympathies for the tradition of necessity, and what [she] had learned about conservation" (3) in her years abroad. In approaching the subject of the cycle, then, the poet feels divided, between two cultures, between old and new, and, more tellingly, within herself. Her emotions pull her one way, intellect and learning another.

The poems in the cycle record the poet's memories of her childhood in Iceland. The image of the "hand that draws . . . /

in" recurs throughout the cycle in ways which reverberate, sometimes ironically, against the sense and tone established by that image in the epigraph. In the second poem of the cycle, for instance, the poet recalls the whaling season:

> men, women and children in the water
> beating in the small whales with bare
> hands, herding them in
> the ocean red with blood as far
> as you looked. (75)

Here the hands which draw in do so bloodily as instruments of death and destruction. This use of the image proves particularly wrenching because, to this point, the poem fashions a sense of communal, even mythic, wholeness, by presenting the activities of the people in terms of great, unchanging cycles. The poet's granduncle rehearses the diurnal cycle: he "rose daily imitating the weak / attempt at sunrise" (75). Larger cycles—seasonal, generational, or historical—inform the actions of the townspeople: "all the men and women rose to one / purpose. to open season, to go / *whaling* they said the way the ancients / went to *viking*" (75). But the hands which draw in the small whales rupture the sense of containment established by the images of natural and historical cycles: as the hands beat in the whales, the ocean turns "red with blood as far / as you looked."

Quite in contrast, in the next poem of the cycle, the poet uses the image of the hand to draw together the human, the animal, and what can only be termed Providence. This poem begins with division: a sense of the enmity between humankind and the natural world. The poet observes the early morning preparations on board a whaling boat and sees "against the lamps / on board the snow flurried / confused and angry" (76). The preparations of the whalers include gearing up against such inclemency. When the poet looks at the sea, she sees "that open / black mouth of storm and / waves" (76) and the "open boat rocking vio- / lently, knocking against the pier" (76). The repeated "open" underscores first the abysmal nature of the sea, and second, the vulnerability of humankind. In the face of this, the poet asks incredulously, "palm of what hand is this" (76), unable to imagine that any benignly providential force balances this world in its hand. But the poet's private observations begin to merge with collective ones, and then with communal recollection to fashion a more benign vision: "slowly we saw," she says,

> the boat glide, the hand
> harpoons and arrows trace out the night
> search for dawn and whale. the rest
> had to be imagined, how
> they didn't see him but sensed
> the huge presence. words
>
> voices i still hear
> telling us the story of how we were
> saved. we could have starved
> to death. it was whale
> that saw us through. i still think
>
> this is the way mythologies are made. (76)

The verbs "glide" and "trace," with their sense of smoothly continuous motion, gauge the shift towards a vision of harmony. Here the hand which seeks to kill paradoxically draws in life, the "whale / that saw us through." The whale drawn in this way comes to represent an almost transcendent force, something not seen but "sensed," a "huge presence" whose sacrificed life keeps a nation alive.

The sensed but not seen life-saving whale reflects the poem's carefully controlled movement away from a world apprehended empirically and individually to a world conceived collectively and at some level beyond sense. There, the whale becomes something to be imagined, to be felt as a presence. Having forged in this way a vision of harmony, wholeness, unity of purpose, the poet withdraws from that vision, separated from it by consciousness. She recollects the story of the "whale / that saw us through," and then, by adding the words "i still think," signals that her understanding cannot rest with, or in, that story. Hers remains a voice distinct from the voices telling the story. She distances herself further from that story of harmony and unity by concluding in the last line of the poem, a line separated from the rest, that "this is the way mythologies are made."

The ninth and last poem in the cycle presents one of those voices which shape the mythology. This voice affirms and makes even more explicit a belief in the whale as an almost transcendent being capable of sacrificing itself to save this small whaling nation. The voice of "uncle stefán" speaks knowingly:

> the truth is, sjana mín, that whales
> are capable of love, uncle stefán
> said who used to pilot the boats be-
> fore his wife asked him to stay
> home, she couldn't take the pain of
> not knowing and his answer then, you do
> everything for your wife. (82)

The last detail establishes "uncle stefán" as one who knows something about the acting out of love. He can therefore speak with assurance of what he has witnessed in the whales:

> the whale knows how it is with us, how
> crops won't grow, clouds won't break
> the herring won't come. he knows when
> the nets are empty and appears instead
> i've seen that huge mass swim towards us
> lift his head before the harpoon
> gun and wait. there was a time it struck me
>
> the men shot. i couldn't have
> done it. absolutely sure he had volunteered
> himself, that's the truth. (82)

Against "uncle stefán's" truth, eloquently and climactically expressed, the poet weighs other truths about the whaling life, remembering "most vividly," for example, "the absence of trawlers on / the banks" (77). She remembers her classmates, the children of whalers, always fearing that "the ship may not return" (77). "[A]bsence is what i remember best," she says, and the "Death" that "seemed so near at hand" (77). And she remembers that sometimes she "dared to imagine what actually / happens" (79) to those who never returned. Such imaginings remain opposed to the kind of imagining, the kind of story-drawing, that produces the myth of the sacrificed and sacrificing whale. Within the cycle, the poet does not come down emphatically on the side of one or another of these "truths." Her insistence, voiced expressly in a couple of poems, implicitly in others, that absence and loss lie at the heart of her remembering, weighs heavily on one's reading of the cycle. Other voices, however, resonate throughout the cycle and the consciousness of the poet to speak powerfully of another story.

The poet's own reading of the poetic cycle, offered in the prose Introduction, bears in telling ways upon the division figured in the poems between a remembering which has at its centre absence and loss, and a re-membering which incorporates notions of harmony and transcendence. In a probably not entirely conscious attempt to bridge that split, the poet re-presents loss as gain, absence as presence. She says that in these poems she focused on the whalers in order to "more accurately depict the emotions with which I grew up" (3). "There was always a sense," she recalls, "of bleakness, a fear of fate, and an overhanging premonition of death" (3). Here we meet the loss, the absence at the centre of her remembered story. The next sentences, however, begin to transform emptiness into the transcendent body of desire:

> What amazes me now is the readiness with which one was willing to accept death, for others as well as oneself.

> It seemed natural to die, and not at all bitter to die young. I felt that this unarticulated fatalism must have some cause, and I sought to discover the reason as I wrote the poems in this cycle. Death-stories abounded in the folklore we were fed as children, but mixed with the terror of mysterious events and dreams was a profound sense of comfort at the thought of going into that warm darkness. (3)

The shift from "bleakness" to warmth, from "fear" to "comfort," from "premonition" to "that warm darkness," signals that re-vision, as well as the poet's desire to make her voice articulate the truths held by the other voices represented in the cycle. Gunnars here does not simply analyze the fatalism which she sees as fundamental to the people of her country, but dramatizes the process of being drawn into that way of apprehending death. Near the start of the paragraph, she says that in the cycle she tried to "reconcile [her] sympathies for the tradition of necessity, and what [she] had learned about conservation" (3) in her years abroad. But in the rest of her commentary on the cycle, Gunnars says nothing further about conservation, focusing instead on what she knows and remembers of the emotional makeup of her nation. In effect, then, she does not discuss, as she implies she will, the reconciliation between sympathies and learning, between emotion and intellect. Yet she does conclude her commentary on a note suggesting she has reached a resolution:

> I think now that a people's emotional makeup is molded by necessity, and the truth is that a fishing nation has to be prepared to accept a certain percentage of deaths on the fishing banks every season. It is a matter of chance who is chosen each time. (4)

The cool voice here, and the earlier voice describing the warm darkness of death, suggest that the writer has not so much resolved the actual tension between emotion and intellect as turned away from that tension, seeking equilibrium within a resolution based on an emotional need to feel at one with the people of her native country. She rests, finally, with the notion of some kind of transcendence. Although the cool conclusion that a certain percentage of deaths can be expected seems unassailably logical and down-to-earth, the word "chosen" conjures images of a transcendent, governing force.

I have focused in some detail on Gunnars' prose commentary because that commentary reveals just how insistently Gunnars feels the pull inwards, the being drawn into a circle. In dramatizing Gunnars' being drawn into the collective fatalism which the poetry ascribes to voices and consciousnesses distinct from that of the poetic persona, the prose commentary reconciles—as the poetry does not—the poetic voice with those other voices. The commentary thus stands in a complex mediating relationship with the poetry. Far from being simple and straightforward exposition, the prose commentary promotes its own competing "truth" about matters raised through the poetry.

Other sections of the prose Introduction stand in similarly complex and telling relationships to the poetry. The commentary on "Wild Waters," for instance, defines Canadian nature and, implicitly, the poet herself. It does so in ways which do not reflect the experience registered in the poetry. The prose points, as does the poetry, to the intensity of the poet's desire for equilibrium, but without accommodating any of the tensions that inform the poems of the cycle, a cycle occasioned by a canoeing trip to Lake of the Woods, Ontario. Says the poet, "If there is anything that epitomizes the nature of Canada, it is the act of silently gliding over such mirror-calm water and hearing the cry of the loon in the night" (1). The image of mirror-calm water points to a vision of Canadian nature as idyllic, with the poet's self reflected as in a mirror image, undisturbed and undisturbing, having realized a kind of stasis. The poems in the cycle similarly express a longing for equilibrium, but they insist also upon the provisional nature of all stasis.

In the first poem of the cycle, for instance, the poet creates line breaks in such a way as to set the desire for permanence (stability, endurance, stasis, rock-solidness) against the reality of change (the dynamic river current). The poem begins on a note of provisionality: "so far the river / has shot by sharp / rocks" (9). By the end of the poem, this deepens into the expectation of a lacerating loss of support: "so far the rock-solid river bottom has not cut me / off, but only so / far" (9). Elsewhere, the poet affirms, with evident pleasure and satisfaction, that this "has been pure white water / wilderness, always" (9). The "always," seeming to modify "has been," underscores the eternality of the scene, its endurance, unchanged through time. The next lines, however, also take "always" as a modifier, producing quite a different effect: "always / roaring rapids a- / head" (9). Change and danger always await, threatening to undermine solidity, threatening to undo structures of eternity. Even the "horizon," which can so readily figure expansiveness, the widening of vistas in time and space, undergoes a "narrowing" to "drops in the rumbling / end: then / the falls" (9) when filtered through the spray of the water.

In the second poem in the cycle, the poet looks for fulfilment in a boundary time, between dark and dawn: "i only wanted / the early dawn, land / of large, soft / water, to awaken before / / morning, the violent / storm, the inclement time / of day" (10). She desires a momentary stasis: "i only wanted to lift the paddle / / a moment upwards / rest it on the gunwhale in / the early hours / / this is all" (10). The use of the past tense shows the moment of rest, of fulfilment, to be unrealized, while the images of boundary time, time which will immediately turn into something else, show such equilibrium to be unrealizable.

The final poem of the cycle represents a kind of petition for stillness and fulfilment. Here the poet states that it is "time now for wild waters / to still" as she imagines a time when "life / becomes an old / friend," when "we take each other / for granted" (11). There is something vaguely disturbing in this vision, however, something which points to exhaustion rather than to fulfilment; the juxtaposition of the words "still, life" signals lifelessness rather than equilibrium. The second half of the poem seems to conclude with an image of stasis, of fully realized presence, but the image is rendered elusive and almost illusory by slippery syntax and by the emphatically placed, final word, "alone." The poem closes with details which recall Gunnars' description, in the prose commentary, of "mirror-calm" water (1). The poet now speaks of gazing into the water: "time / now for silence, to watch / the underwater weeds bend / waver by themselves, to be / alone" (11). This water seems to yield a reflection of the speaker which promises stasis and fulfilment ("time / now . . . / . . . to be"), but the ambiguous syntax makes it possible to take "underwater weeds" as the subject of "to be," in which case the poet remains unreflected, unfulfilled, unrealized. In either of the readings permitted by the syntax, "alone," set off from the body of the poem, turns the infinitive "to be" to other purposes, making it more a statement of isolation and solitude than of fulfilment and presence.

ii

The poetry of "Wild Waters" and "The Silent Hand" contains tensions not registered or accommodated in the poet's prose commentaries on these cycles, so the prose commentaries promote visions to compete with those in the poetry. This points to one of the more revealing features of *Night Workers*: it is not simply that each commentary stands in this complex relationship to the cycle it analyzes, but that, taken as a whole, the Introduction to *Night Workers* assumes the shape—in a way the poetry of the volume does not—of the poet's desire for wholeness and coherence. The discrete commentaries in the Introduction thus join to form a story of the poet's assumption of a vocational identity within which she can apprehend and give voice to what she comes to call "the truth" (4). The Introduction accomplishes this in spite of the poet's own disclaimer near the start. There she says that, while the poems in the volume "register a search for a kind of truth . . . imbedded in place," she is afraid that "this book of poems amounts to a record of what [she] did not find" (1). One can trace in the commentaries a coherent progression, from the poet's expression of relief at being freed from an old mould (paragraph on "Wild Waters" [1]), to her tacit assumption of an almost vatic role (paragraph on "The Night Workers of Ragnarök" [4]). In the course of the Introduction, the poet implicitly likens her role to that of theologians, who do not seek empirical truth (paragraph on "Milky Way Vegetation" [1-2]). Accordingly, she presents her journey to the home of a poetic mentor in the religious image of a "pilgrimage" (paragraph on "Stone Bridge Poems" [2]). She sets against her mentor's pioneering "urge" to press forward her own need to gaze backwards, to recover personal and social pasts, and sets against the mentor's fondness for the unknown of geographical frontiers her own attraction to a transcendent unknown, that "warm darkness" (3) she speaks about in her commentary on "The Silent Hand." In the end, she resolves that, like Rousseau, she understands her " 'function is to tell the truth, [if] not to make people believe it' " (4).

In developing its own vision, the prose Introduction to *Night Workers* becomes an integral part of the poetic volume, for it enters into a very active dialectical relationship with the poetry. I have chosen to focus on this aspect of the volume for several reasons. First, the vision which emerges from the Introduction is one of wholeness and coherence, and one which fashions a vatic role for the poet. This points to the intensity of the poet's desire to be drawn in, to be defined, to be located. The Introduction forges this vision in spite of the fact that the poetry it introduces remains fraught with tensions and ambivalences which shatter wholeness, dislocating the poet, both from herself and from the world.

Second, the fractured self and world assume wholeness

again in the volume's Introduction, in what many would take to be marginal, or extra-literary space. This anticipates, I think, subsequent directions in Gunnars' work, specifically the kind of thing Gunnars attempts in *The Prowler*, a work very tentatively identified on the dust jacket as "a novel."[1] In *The Prowler*, the writer's highly self-conscious commentary becomes, formally and thematically, an explicit part of the fiction which addresses story-telling, forging wholeness out of the dislocated pieces of a writer's life.

iii

Gunnars' work offers fertile ground for exploring some of the issues which occupy much post-structuralist criticism. For example, deconstructive theory sees "God" and "self" as "metaphysical concepts," not "real" entities, but concepts constructed out of the play of signifiers and signifieds inside levels of discourse. There can therefore be no unified individual "self" who transcends space and time, only multiple selves incarnated through different levels of discourse. Not one of these levels can be privileged over the others as a discourse of The Truth. The deconstructive denial of a unified self contrasts with Gunnars' assertion of such a self in her prose Introduction. For Gunnars' Introduction to *Night Workers* shows her, above all, fashioning herself and writing as a "self" which implicitly claims to transcend the vicissitudes of history and geography. This act claims a privileged position for her as a subject, even as it claims a privileged position for her prose over her poetry. Gunnars calls her volume of poems a record of what she did not find in her search for a "truth embedded in place" (1). But over this record of loss, she inscribes a search for a self within which to ground the "truth" she wishes to "tell" (4).

---

1 The words "a novel" are printed on the front of the dust jacket, alongside the title, but in a line parallel to the spine of the book.

Because this autonomous, unified self appears in a prose commentary, in a seemingly extra-literary space, it claims for itself a certain stability, a certain resistance to the kind of fragmentation of self registered (and, indeed, in light of the long-established conventions of lyrical poetry, expected) in the poems. But beneath appearances, various features of the privileged prose commentary betray the actual fictionality of the self presented there. For one thing, the self of the Introduction remains very much a textual one, defined intertextually in relation to other texts, most notably the *Confessions* of Jean-Jacques Rousseau. Gunnars forges her vatic role out of a series of intertextual allusions to Rousseau's work. In other ways, too, the self of this prose commentary seems to be a "constructed" one. For example, to trace her use of words and tropes having to do with sight, with looking, would be to trace a self-referentiality which permits no escape to a realm outside of discourse.

The kind of double pull evident in the Introduction to *Night Workers*, where Gunnars wishes to define a transcendent self, but does so in a discourse which remains irredeemably "textual," becomes more evident still in *The Prowler*. In that "novel," Gunnars consistently denies the possibility that there can be a "story" of her life, yet she proceeds insistently to fashion one.

Gunnars' works to date have grown increasingly autobiographical in cast. The tensions and tendencies I have sketched here suggest that, increasingly, her works question the possibility of an autonomous, unified self, which reveals that she deals with a key problematic of our time.

Works Cited

Gunnars, Kristjana. *The Night Workers of Ragnarök*. Toronto: Press Porcépic, 1985.

__________. *The Prowler*. Red Deer: Red Deer College Press, 1989.

Hjartarson, Paul. "Transformation of the 'I': Self and Community in the Poetry of Kristjana Gunnars." *Lund Studies in English* 78 (1988): 123-37.

Robert Kroetsch's *Seed Catalogue*: The Deconstruction of the Meta-narrative of the Cowboy

David Arnason

The man on a horse, riding off into the sunset, is the quintessential Western image of the masculine, and perhaps the final fantasy of patriarchal culture. In *Seed Catalogue*, Robert Kroetsch sets out to deconstruct the meta-narrative[1] of the cowboy, and by so doing to show the failure of patriarchal culture, particularly in its relationship with art, and more particularly in its relationship with writing. I use the term "writing" not only in its ordinary sense of the literary arts,

---

1 By the term "meta-narrative" I mean a major narrative that is behind specific instances of cultural practice. Thus, in this essay, I use the story of the "cowboy" as the general story behind certain specific instances of masculine behaviour. In other instances we might speak of the meta-narrative of the "princess" or the "movie star" to explicate instances of female behaviour. On a larger scale, we may speak of the meta-narrative of "progress" as an informing narrative behind all North American cultural practices. These larger narratives are sometimes spoken of as "myths" but I wish to avoid that term because of the religious and universalist notions that are often attached to it.

but also in the Derridean sense of writing as the sign of a sign, writing as supplement.[2]

Seed Catalogue is in no way an innocent text. Kroetsch has written a poem that at the same time works as an elaborate post-structural critical essay. The language and the concepts of the Derridean philosophy of deconstruction are everywhere in the text: presence, absence, trace, palimpsest, erasure. Everywhere, supplementarity reveals the duplicity and the lack of apparent wholes: in love, sexuality, nature, masculinity, even in language itself.

Yet for all its intelligence, *Seed Catalogue* is no more immune to a duplicitous reading than any other text. The original version of the poem was printed on a ten percent screen of pages from the Mackenzie Seed catalogue from which portions of the poem are drawn, a sort of palimpsest that declares the poem to be out of phase with itself. And of course it is, but in a less obvious way than that. For all the temptations to read the poem as socio-cultural criticism or psycho-biographical confession, *Seed Catalogue* remains itself. As Derrida says of Rousseau,

> Yet if reading is not to be content with doubling the text, it cannot legitimately transgress the text toward something other than it, toward a referent (a reality that is metaphysical, historical, psychobiographical, etc.) or toward a signified outside the text whose content could take place, could have taken place outside language, that is to say, in the sense that we give here to that word, outside of writing in general. (158)

In other words, as Derrida goes on to say, "*There is nothing outside of the text; il n'y a pas de hors-texte*" (158). It is the

---

2 The text which most interests me in this respect is Jacques Derrida's *Of Grammatology*, first published in English in 1976. *Seed Catalogue* first appeared in 1977. The similarity between certain of Derrida's and Kroetsch's ideas is striking.

same for Kroetsch. Outside his horse-text there can be no *hors-texte*.

Kroetsch has speculated on the man on horseback as the basic image of masculine presence and power in Western (i.e. prairie) writing. In a paper on Willa Cather and Sinclair Ross, he shows how the horse/house images define male and female presence. The man on horseback is masculine, phallic and free. The woman in the enveloping and enclosing female space of the house awaits the unseating of the rider. The horseman must be unhorsed and housed, domesticated, tamed. Kroetsch says:

> The basic grammatical pair in the story-line (the energy-line) of prairie fiction is horse:house. To be on a horse is to move:motion into distance. To be in a house is to be fixed:a centering unto stasis. Horse is masculine. House is feminine. Horse:house. Masculine: feminine. On:in. Motion:stasis. ("Fear" 49)

Kroetsch faces a dilemma in *Seed Catalogue*'s deconstruction of the meta-narrative of Western North American male culture: the site of artistic creation is a female site,[3] the site of the garden, the site inhabited by the mother who is also Nature. Natural fecundity, growth and creation, and by extension, artistic creativity partake of the feminine. And yet the energy that fuels the creation is masculine, the energy of the seed.

In particular, note that what is catalogued is seeds, not eggs. The catalogue is a mail order/male ordering. Historically, taxonomy, division, and order have been male categories, male enterprises. What the catalogue provides is not real vegetables but writing about vegetables, a supplement to vegetables that precedes the vegetables themselves. Accordingly, the vegetables come described in a language of hierarchy and order. The cabbage is "in every respect a

---

3 A position which Kroetsch takes in a number of his works.

thoroughbred, a **cabbage** of **highest pedigree**" (*Seed Catalogue* 11). The cauliflower is "one of the **greatest inheritances** of the **present generation**" (29). Everywhere, we encounter the language of male order: breeding, pedigree, inheritance.

So how do you grow a poet, if that poet is to be male and the site of artistic creativity is female? You feminize him. All poets are sissies. As a man-child in the garden, he falls from his horse, the first fortunate fall for the artist:

> You've got to understand this:
> I was sitting on the horse.
> The horse was standing still.
> I fell off. (11)

The hired man, the supplement to the father, cannot understand this fall from manhood because it is a static fall, a passive female fall and not an active male fall:

> The hired man laughed: how
> in hell did you manage to
> fall off a horse that was
> *standing still?* (11)

The mother understands, of course. She whispers the unspeakable, incestuous, erotic invitation. "Bring me the radish seeds, / my mother whispered" (11). It is an equivocal invitation into sexuality and art, because it is also an invitation to death. She whispers the words once more, but this time from the grave, while "the Cincinnati Reds were playing the Detroit Tigers" (15). The male games go on even at the death of the mother. The mother is always dangerous. To refuse the Oedipal separation, to give in to the mother's invitation and bring her the radish seeds means to languish in what Lacan calls the "imaginary stage," the time of pure pleasure before the emergence of a self. And selflessness, of course, is death.

The point becomes clear near the end of the poem.

Poet, teach us
to love our dying.[4] (45)

Seed Catalogue's concern with writing, both as art and as supplement to oral speech, the sign of a sign, leads it on the one hand to relate the written to the oral, and on the other to identify writing-as-supplement with sexuality. At the first level, the text plays off the apparently oral with the apparently written; "apparently" because all of the text is a written text, even that part which proclaims its orality through a series of markers. Part 2 of the poem tells the story of the father's relationship with the badger. Here the text mimics the rhythms of oral speech: "My father was mad at the badger: the badger was digging holes in the potato patch, threatening man and beast with broken limbs (I quote)" (17). The reduction of the level of diction to a vernacular "mad at" and the

4 These lines invite a psychoanalytic as well as a deconstructive reading. Kroetsch's aesthetic seems to identify art with murder and death, with coming to what Julia Kristeva calls the thetic boundary, the line between what she calls the symbolic and the semiotic. At the level of the semiotic (Lacan's imaginary which precedes the mirror stage) the drives are free and anarchic. Language is a defensive system which channels the drives through the signifier. It protects the body from the attack of the drives by making it possible for the body to signify itself through positions. In that sense, the death drive underlies all language.

At the same time, language serves the death drive by providing a point of narcissism toward which the drive can be directed. That point is, of course, the self. Whatever psychoanalytic model we use to explain the rupture of language (Freud's Oedipal prohibition which generates the reality principle, Lacan's mirror stage that leads from the imaginary stage to the symbolic stage, or Kristeva's movement from the semiotic to the thetic) we are led to the same position. The self-aware subject is forever trapped on a boundary between the drives and language. The split self (subject/object) constructed out of language is a defence against death. But poetry, as a disturbance of the signifying chain, is a manifestation of the death drive. The poetic is a surplus, a supplement to the death drive which the mirror could not contain.

catch-phrase "threatening man and beast" function to mark oral speech. A lyric interlude follows:

Love is an amplification
by doing / over and over.

Love is a standing up
to the loaded gun.

Love is a burrowing. (17)

Here, the spacing on the page, the tropes, rhythms and italics, all point to the written, the domain of the poet, the site of supplementarity. The badger, the "little man" (17) of the story, has an odd, androgynous sexuality. He stands up to the phallic "loaded gun," yet he burrows into the female earth. (The phrase "little man" is also a subtle way of referring to the clitoris.)[5]

Of course, the apparently oral and the stylistically poetic are both written, part of writing in general, pure supplement. But the duplicitous text invites a false division, an "oral" writing set off against a "written" writing, sponsored by what Dennis Cooley has called "the vernacular muse." And of course the oral comes off as more honest, somehow more democratic and therefore more "true."[6] *Seed Catalogue* is characterized by a series of carefully coded "oral" passages ("shit / we're up against it" [29]) and this has led, in spite of its manifest deconstruction of myths of male power, and its pessimism about male possibility, to some readers seeing the text as a celebration of male energy. They are not entirely

5 Usually "the little man in the boat."

6 Speech is traditionally regarded as prior to writing, a first-order signifying process in which the phoneme, because it declares the presence of the speaking subject, precedes the grapheme which only stands in for it. Much of Derrida's work can be understood as an argument against this position. And of course the distinction is particularly blurred when writing re-presents speech.

deceived in that one-sided reading, since the text itself is deliberately ambiguous about its own meaning.

Seed Catalogue describes a second fall in "the other garden" (37), the garden of the other. The text questions, "*But how do you grow a lover?*" (19). The answer is the old one. You get thrown out of Eden. "This is the God's own truth," the priest tells his catechism class, "playing dirty is a mortal sin" (19). The priest, defender of patriarchy in its Christian form, throws the children out of the garden of their sexual innocence, and he does it with language:

> he had named it   he had named
> our world   out of existence (21)

That act of naming, of cataloguing sin, of defining by taxonomy imposes male patriarchal order and guarantees its resulting guilt. This truth, the possession of the Christian patriarchal God ("the God's own truth" [19]), is spoken to a "son." The sentence is "Son. For penance, keep your peter in your pants for the next thirteen years" (21). Sexual abstinence is ordered, and the libidinal consequences, as acted out in the text, are severe. In case the parallel is not clear, the text reminds us: "Adam and Eve got drownded" (21).

One aspect of the libidinal consequence of the double fall in the two gardens is expressed in the elaborate joke about masturbation in section 5. The duplicitous text brings together two chains of substitutions, the sexual and the linguistic, and merges them. At the sexual level, the mother in the garden has functioned as a substitution for Mother Nature, and Germaine, the appropriately named sexual other, has served as a substitute for the mother. After the priest's necessary Oedipal forbidding of the sexual relationship and his demand for abstinence, the final sexual recourse is masturbation. By preferring the sign of the thing rather than the thing itself, the narrator saves himself from death, or to be more precise, he saves himself from the loss of self that would result from refusing the Oedipal rupture. ("Bring me the radish seeds," the mother whispers from the grave [11].) But the apparent success of this egotistical economy is a wounding of the self by the self, and a fatal expenditure of seed. Within the framework of moral representation of *Seed Catalogue*, sterility is disastrous for the lover, gardener, and poet.

The same sort of disastrous sterility faces the gardener: "I planted some melons, just to see what would / happen. Gophers ate everything" (27). For the poet it is the same:

> I applied to the Government.
> I wanted to become a postman,
> to deliver real words
> to real people.
>
> There was no one to receive
> my application. (27)

Gardens which fail to grow and writing which is not delivered are like the seed that masturbation wastes.

Writing and sexuality come together in the joke, only the punch line of which is delivered in the poem. The joke, relatively well known among young males in Western Canada, is worth the re-telling here since *Seed Catalogue*'s intertextual relationship with this absent text is important. A young boy is caught masturbating in the graveyard by a priest. The priest orders him to stop: "If you do that, you'll die," the priest tells him, and leaves. The boy slowly continues his masturbation, saying to himself, "If I do this, I'll die. If I do this I'll die." Then, in response to his own oncoming orgasm, he moves to the formula, "I don't give a damn if I do die do die do die do die . . ." (27), and on, presumably, to bliss.

The joke has certain interesting parallels with the text of *Seed Catalogue*. A priest forbids sexuality. The setting in the graveyard metonymically associates the auto-erotic event with death. The command meets resistance. ("We decided we could do it / just one last time" [21].) Most importantly, the repetitions of the words "do die" in the joke push language beyond usual lexical meaning.[7] Just as the actual onanistic act seeks to supplement an originary sexual act,[8] so the writing moves to pure babble, to an ideal Rousseauean prelinguistic origin. The poem repeats the phrase "do die" twenty-two and a half times, far more than enough to make its point in the joke, but only as much as seems necessary to push the sentence beyond meaning and into a representation of pure, originary language.

The Oedipal prohibitions that circumscribe and control sexuality are paralleled in the text by the father's prohibition of poetry. The father, in tightly controlled and precise sarcastic language, describes the tools needed for barbed-wire fencing. In a passage ambiguously shifted to the left, but still presumably his, the father describes patriarchal authoritarian ordering:

> We give form to this land by running
> a series of posts and three strands
> of barbed wire around a ¼-section. (31)

Having asserted the primacy of male order, he adds, "And the next time you want to / write a poem / we'll start the haying" (31). A little later the poem quotes Rudy Wiebe: "You must lay great black steel lines of fiction, break up that space with huge design . . ." (33). Wiebe echoes the father's prohibition and follows his own prohibition, "no song can do that . . ." (33), with a demonstration of phallogocentric lyricism. On February 14, 1976, Valentine's Day, he takes the community ("Lorna & Byrna, Ralph & Steve and me" [33]) to the appropriately named Oldman River to show them where the Crees murdered the Bloods (whose names metonymically

---

7 I refer to the well-known phenomenon that a phrase, consistently repeated, tends to become babble.

8 Even sexual intercourse itself can be understood as supplement, standing in for the authentic presence of the other.

conjure their bloody deaths) in a kind of masculine erotic violence. Afterwards he shows them "Rilke's word / *Lebensgliedes*" (33), shows them, that is, the "life-member," the phallus.[9]

It is not surprising then that the older poet, unable to stay forever in his mother's loving arms because to stay in the Imaginary is death, and unable to achieve originary grace through masturbation because to do so is to immorally spill his mortal seed, failing, in other words, to find a supplement that will complete his original creative impulse, must "deliver the pain to some woman" (39). There is no way to refuse what Lacan calls the phallus, to escape the phallocentric symbolic, to live, that is, outside language, before language.

Drunk with Al Purdy at the Chateau Lacombe, he celebrates the masculine. In the phallic tower in the centre of the world, even the Edmonton winter is not enough "to cool our out-sights" (35), take the heat from phallic rifles, and Purdy, still a cowboy, even "galloped a Cariboo horse right straight through the dining area" (35). Later, the poet-narrator is not so sure. Drunk again, this time in the Toronto airport, the poet, in a parody of medieval romance, introduces the knight and the lady. The lady is the woman at the end of the bar. The knight is Pete Knight, "King of All Cowboys, Bronc-Busting Champion of the World" (39). Like the poet, he has fallen off his horse, and in his case the result is death.

The masculine impulse reaches its farthest point of violence in the war, and in the person of "my cousin who was

---

9 Daniel Lenoski, in a note to the edition of *Seed Catalogue* in *a / long prairie lines*, points out that Rilke only used the word once in his work. (See *Sämtliche Werke*, ed. E. Zinn et al., Vol. 2: 435.) He includes a translation of the passage, by Claus Lappe:

> And suddenly the girl picking roses
> Grabs hold of the full bud of his life-member [Lebensgliedes]
> And with the fright of the difference
> The gentle gardens in her fade. (Lenoski 130)

shot down while bombing the city that was his maternal great-grandmother's birthplace" (43). He becomes:

> : a
> strange
>
> man/falling
> on the city. (43)

This is Germany, and Kroetsch evokes the figure of Icarus falling from the sky in the painting by Breughel. Icarus is the final symbol of male arrogance, the man who flew too close to the sun, that image of patriarchal power. The feminine again appears in the form of "A strange muse: forgetfulness. Feeding her far children to ancestral guns, blasting them out of the sky, smack/ into the earth. Oh, she was the mothering sort. Blood/ on her green thumb" (43). The feminine seems as violent as the masculine, but the inversion is more apparent than real. The muse, though represented as female, is always in fact male inspiration, sexuality at the service of the phallus.

Two final images of the feminine bring the poem to its ambiguous close. In a quiet lyric passage, Kroetsch evokes the mother who teaches the son the simple details of prairie life, in particular, teaches him to recognize his own body, "the smell / of my sweating armpits" (45). Finally, a "found" letter evokes an idyllic moment. Amie, presumably a personification of love, tethers a mare, Cindy, the horse as female, to a truck near Brooks, Alberta, the appropriate place for a baptismal rebirth. An ambiguous "we" lies down in the back of the truck on some Brome grass, which, like the poet, "*Flourishes. / Under absolute neglect*" (37). The passage is quiet, gentle, suggesting a closure that never happens. At the end of the poem nothing has been resolved. Adam and Eve, the first male and the first female, have "*got drownded*" (47). The poem refuses closure, and ends with the question "*Who was left?*" (47).

Seed Catalogue offers more than a deconstruction of the

aesthetic of the cowboy. It looks, in a broader sense, at the entire cultural situation of the writer in the Canadian west. In answer to the question "*How do you grow a past/* to live in" (23) the text details a long list of absences. These absences constitute the story of Western civilization, conjuring philosophers, poets, cultural practices and instruments, science, technology and monuments. At the same time, Kroetsch subverts the high seriousness of his own list by including another series of sexual and scatological absences which are in fact the presences of a prairie past. The result is an ambiguous statement. The phallic energy of the subversive absences (the girl who has promised to allow the speaker to kiss her nipples in the foyer of the Palliser Hotel [25]) reduces the value of the serious cultural artifacts. But that energy does not seem sufficient to displace them. Negative traces of a past that was once a present are negative precisely in that they locate the past as elsewhere. But other than the libidinal energy of the text, delivered in a language coded as oral and vernacular, there are no traces of a past that was once a present in *this* place.

When the text sets out to define the poet by starting with an invocation, it stammers into silence:

> Start: with an invocation
> invoke—
>
> His muse is
> his muse/if
> memory is (29)

In a place without history, without cultural memory, how can the poet function? The text conjures a series of female figures who might serve as muses. "That girl / you felt up in the / school barn" [29], "that / girl you necked with / out by Hastings' slough" [29] and the "girl in the skating / rink" [29]) are all offered as possibilities, but each ends up as a sexual object and not as a source of inspiration.

In the practice of Derridean deconstruction, everything leaves its trace, the sign of an absence that declares presence. In this text, however, the poet leaves "no trace of his coming / or going" (33) except for a "scarred" page, with the implication that his writing has merely defaced paper with a "spoor of wording" (33), with the implication that the writing is a trace of an animal. Finally, his writing is no more than a pile of rabbit turds, a kind of excretory function that accidentally maps the landscape. "*West is a winter place*" (45), the poet tells us. There, "*The palimpsest of prairie / under the quick erasure / of snow, invites a flight*" (45). The traces of a prairie landscape and a prairie culture are put under erasure (*sur rasure*) by the coming of winter, and the artist is invited to flee the place.

Kroetsch's *Seed Catalogue* examines only one side of the binary he himself articulates. It is all horse, no house. The house may be defined as "the home place," but there is no entry to it. Talking about the figure of the artist in Cather's and Ross's work, Kroetsch says,

> The male, certainly, to make his radical beginning, takes on the role of the orphan or cowboy or outlaw. He approaches the female. He approaches the garden. He approaches the house. . . . And only then does he realize he has defined himself out of all entering. ("Fear" 55)

The house, the static space of the female and at the same time the site of the creative, is unavailable to the male artist. There are no women in the poem. There are only good mothers, Earth Mothers, muses, earth goddesses, waitresses, cooks, and potential lovers, all the figures of male fantasy, all male creations of the feminine. Woman, the Female, has only a textual signification. There is no "real" house, no "real" Woman to authenticate, to authorize a beginning for the artist, that is to say, no *hors texte*.

Seed Catalogue is also, however, pure horse-text, the male poetic ridden out, written out, wrung out. But that male poetic was never possible anyway. The poet had fallen from the horse that was standing still before the text began. Adam and Eve, first Man and first Woman, are "drownded." And so, with neither the masculine nor the feminine, the question remains "who was left?" The ambiguous text does not offer an answer, but it leaves a suggestion: only the poet, the scriptor, the occasion of writing and the text, *Seed Catalogue*, present trace of a past quest to find a poetic for the prairies.

Works Cited

Cooley, Dennis. *The Vernacular Muse: The Eye and Ear in Contemporary Literature*. Winnipeg: Turnstone Press, 1987.

Derrida, Jacques. ". . . That Dangerous Supplement . . ." *Of Grammatology*. 1976. Baltimore: Johns Hopkins University Press, 1977.

Kroetsch, Robert. "The Fear of Women in Prairie Fiction." *Robert Kroetsch: Essays*. Ed. Frank Davey and bpNichol. *Open Letter*. 5th ser. 4 (Spring 1983).

________. *Seed Catalogue*. Winnipeg: Turnstone Press, 1977.

Lenoski, Daniel S., ed. *a / long prairie lines: An Anthology of Long Prairie Poems*. Winnipeg: Turnstone Press, 1989.

Zinn, E., et al., eds. *Sämtliche Werke*. Wiesbaden: Insel-Verlag, 1966. Vol. 2.

Sandra Birdsell's *Agassiz Stories*: Speaking the Gap

Charlene Diehl-Jones

Sandra Birdsell's stories, collected together in *Agassiz Stories*, piece themselves together into a kind of mosaic: shards of experience bump up against one another, or overlap, or begin again at some distance; characters and incidents appear and reappear in different configurations, from different vantage points. Birdsell offers "no climactic finish, no solution, no particular protagonist" (Spalding 28). Instead, a mosaic of bits, of impressions, a mosaic of stories that admits incompleteness, partiality, gaps, silences, even as it insinuates overarching patterns. As in Alice Munro's *Lives of Girls and Women*, as in Margaret Laurence's *A Bird in the House*, Birdsell's stories "require their surrounding stories, so that the real narrative 'unit' . . . is the fragmented whole" (New 102). And within individual stories, Birdsell resists a "straight-line sort of story-telling" (McCormack 13). Smaller-scale mosaics of bits, of impressions.

This structure of (restructured) fragments cues Birdsell's concerns, both aesthetic and thematic/political: she explores edges, gaps, margins; she explores the tremendous power imbedded in our complex system of master narratives—cultural, social, economic, religious, sexual—power that presses those at the margins toward isolation, toward silence, toward invisibility. Text as bricolage,[1] cobbling together another configuration, another version of the world, from material already at hand. Admitting gaps and seams, admitting rash relocatings. Text as subversive challenge, borrowing wholesale from the tradition that denies it voice, exposing gaps where none are admitted.[2]

Birdsell's stories speak into the gap, speak out of the gap. She writes of children, of Métis, of Mennonites, of the working

---

1 Claude Levi-Strauss, in *The Savage Mind*, explores the strategies of the bricoleur, locating them opposite the engineer's:

> The 'bricoleur' is adept at performing a large number of diverse tasks; but, unlike the engineer, he does not subordinate each of them to the availability of raw materials and tools conceived and procured for the purpose of the project. His universe of instruments is closed and the rules of his game are always to make do with 'whatever is at hand'. . . . [T]he engineer is always trying to make his way out of and go beyond the constraints imposed by a particular state of civilization while the 'bricoleur' by inclination or necessity always remains within them. (17-19)

2 In *Recodings: Art, Spectacle, Cultural Politics*, Hal Foster argues that those relegated to the margins, those labelled 'other' by virtue of economic/social/cultural (under)development, or conflicting ideology, or sex, can appropriate strategies of bricolage to subvert the oppressive order, to (ex)pose the possibility that "western culture is hardly the integral 'engineered' whole that it seems to be but that it too is *bricolé*" (201). Textual gaps, then, become politically potent, positing another way of constructing the world and relations between people. Foster: "myth is a one-way appropriation, an act of power, while *bricolage* is a process of textual play, of loss and gain: whereas myth abstracts and pretends to the natural, *bricolage* cuts up, makes concrete, delights in the artificial—it knows no identity, stands for no pretense of presence or universal guise for relative truths" (201). Bricolage offers the woman writer a strategy for speaking against the 'myth' of patriarchal power, the master narratives that appropriate her voice(s) and her place(s) in the world.

class. She writes especially of women.[3] Her characters feel the exquisite pain of isolation, of silencing; they also insist on surviving, reaching out, and, tentatively, tentatively, speaking themselves into existence in a world that discourages dialogue.

The book opens with Maurice, alone, surveying a flooded world in which familiar landmarks are submerged, hidden, lost. An unfamiliar world. A world of silence which he breaks "because he needed to hear the sound of his own voice" (3). The isolation unsettles him, makes him anxious; he craves reassurance that "he was not the only human being left in the world" (4). In his sense of aloneness, of being (left) on the edge of a world he cannot quite recognize, cannot quite engage, in his anxiety at being wrapped in silence, Maurice claims kinship with the characters who follow him in these stories: all sense, with varying degrees of rage, frustration, fear, despair, their own isolation. Caught in the gap. Truda on Toronto Street, "the feeling of being invisible" (315) increasingly acute in her new surroundings, desperately willing the student across the street to "Look at me. . . . Lift up your head for once" (314). Betty unable, finally, to tell the Wednesday Circle of Mr. Joy's sexual overtures, recognizing her misplaced faith in the power of their community, "the promise of their womanly strength" (52), their capacity for honesty and compassion. Dave Reimer and Rocky, his son, sharing their abandoned grain elevator home with heat, with rats, with fear, with hopelessness, stowaways in "the bowels of [a]

---

3 Though Birdsell writes powerfully, even predominantly, of women, tracing matrilineal lines of influence—Mika through her daughters and granddaughters—her stories do not fit comfortably within the parameters of feminist writing: she tends, like Margaret Laurence before her, to locate oppression/repression as an experience of class as well as of gender. My reading of her work, then, is not explicitly feminist, though a focus on silencing, on marginalization, and on strategies for countering those pressures, announces an alliance, a kinship of concerns.

creaking ship" (176). Lureen, collecting calendars, writing "on the backs of the spent time" (206) a child's messages to an uncertain future. Mika. Elizabeth, her sister. Grandmother Thiessen. Laurence Anderson. Henry Schultz. David Pankratz. Birdsell's characters live on the edges, uncertain of their connection with their parents and grandparents, their siblings, their neighbours, their friends, their society, their religion. Their dreams are at once simple and elusive: they imagine survival, belonging, community, communication; they imagine speaking themselves out of the margins.

It is perhaps this powerful instinct for survival that moves us most as readers of these stories. Our own anxieties, focused by distance, focused by proximity. Our own several strategies for coping, too. Some of these characters react with anger, defying the forces that constrain them. Lureen, lashing out at her mother, her grandfather, the bus driver, overwhelmed with anger about a "world dangling like a bauble about to shatter on the floor" (206): " 'Have you ever thought,' " she asks the mysterious angel-traveller, " 'that at this very moment, someone may be pressing a button and that the world may come to an end? And we'll all be instant cooked weiners [sic]?' " (211). Lureen, aching inside: "I am hoping to get through life, but I don't think I will" (210). Anger, defiance. Mika, "as defenseless as a badger" (34), flies into a rage at Betty's indiscretions with Laurence and spends a day making a rock garden instead of mothering her children (and husband). Her responsibilities seem pointless, thankless—" 'Alright, okay. You can't change a thing. No amount of harping will change anything. They'll do what they want to do in the end anyway. I'm butting my head against a stone wall' " (72)—and they wear her down: " 'I'm always in the family way. And I'm tired. I'm tired of being a mother' " (73). Mika's anger: her response to crippling by forces as powerful as they are abstract. The pressures of a patriarchal family structure, an equally patriarchal religious structure, a difficult economic situation, leave her exhausted, frustrated, hemmed in by demands that disallow her exploration of herself as person, as woman, outside her assigned roles. Great gaps of self. Silenced by expectation, silenced by fear.

Mika in her anger lashes out, but tends to strike those more weak, more constrained to the margins, than she is herself. The silenced becoming the silencer. To shy Truda: " 'Look at this mess, will you? You can't keep these drawings forever. The wax in the crayons will attract mice' " (35); " 'Where did you ever get all the paper?' she asked. She was practical, wondered more about the gathering of paper rather than why or what was in the drawings" (36). To pregnant Betty:

> "Listen. . . . It's going to hurt. Like menstrual cramps, only a hundred times worse; as it should. But if you keep the baby, the trouble only begins. Children are a constant pain." . . . She led Betty into the bedroom and gathered several limp cotton smocks from the back of the closet and pushed them down into a shopping bag in a furtive way as though they were shameful depressing items. "Be sensible. Don't ruin your life," she said. "Give it up."
>
> "I don't know," Betty said.
>
> "Well, do what you want, but don't bring it home to me," Mika said. (170)

With Lureen:

> "Well, how should I know where it is, you look for it." Mika's voice was raised suddenly, shattering the peacefulness. . . .
>
> "I did look for it," Lureen answered.
>
> "Must I come?" It was a threat.
>
> Lureen's tone matched her mother's. "I said I looked and so I did. I'm not lying."
>
> "Alright then, I'll come," Mika said and Maurice heard her feet slap angrily across the kitchen floor. "But I'm warning you, if I find that shoe of yours, I'll give you

> such a smack for not looking for it properly. You have to get down on your knees when you look. You searched high and low, eh? We'll see about that." (29)

Mika, speaking out of frustration, out of anger, "as serious as a mousetrap" (68), and as ready to spring. Her anger with Maurice—her outrage at his casual assumption of her presence as mother and homemaker, his insistence on a life for himself outside the home, at the barbershop, at the pub—makes her particularly cutting; she compounds the silencing he experiences in the community:

> She'd denied him the presence of his brothers in his own home. She was going to teach the children to speak German. "Fine. And what should we teach them of my background?"
>
> Her tightly contained anger broke loose. Her eyes became pinpoints of hostility. "What would you teach them?" she asked, spitting the words at him overtop the baby's head. "How to drink?"
>
> "Listen here, my grandfather was a river man."
>
> "I thought you said he came from Quebec."
>
> "On my mother's side, I mean."
>
> "That must have been before I came," she said. She dismissed anything that had happened before she'd come to Canada as being unimportant, not affecting her in any way. (32)

Mika is not alone in bludgeoning with her anger: Maurice, loosened by drink, becomes infuriated, and though "he'd wanted to smash into her breasts with his fists . . . instead, he'd taken her with force, without using precautions, with a grinding punishing force that he felt in his own muscles this morning" (31). Pressure toward isolation. Silencing. The pathos, and richness, of Birdsell's characters: they are not only victims of a dehumanizing system, but are also agents of their own and each other's unhappiness. Contributors. Caught in the act, caught in the gap.

Under extreme pressure toward silence, toward isolation, one's options narrow. To choose silence rather than to be coerced into impotence. Betty's anxious retreat from an essay: "there is too much to say about the wild plum tree. The assignment has paralyzed her" (113). Maurice's anxious retreat from age and ill health: "he saw the picture of a man locked inside a body that had given out on him, a living death. . . . What would be worse? He pulled the trigger and felt the hot path of metal through the roof of his mouth. The choice was his" (145). Truda, terrified in a strange place during the flood, making a "vow not to speak" (42):

> "Guess what, Truda? You have a new baby brother. I've named him Peter. Isn't that wonderful?" Static on the telephone wire, it was the sparrows bouncing on the wire outside the window, making Mika's words break into fragments . . . guess . . . baby . . . wonder. . . .
>
> I said. I said. I said. I said. The sparrows one after another fluttered from the wire. It shivered, a silver arc, then it straightened and dissolved into the sky. Silence.
>
> I said, don't leave me here. When are you coming to get me?
>
> "Have you got nothing to say? Cat's got your tongue?"
>
> "Don't worry, it's a little thing," the farm woman said. "Once you come she'll find her tongue again." (42-43)

Truda, sensing that "words were traps" (36), struggling to function, to cope. Even as an adult, hiding inside too-ample flesh. Insulated. Isolated.

A more subtle and complex strategy of silencing oneself and at the same time finding oneself a voice involves assuming another's voice and language. Elizabeth's world turns over when her husband suffers a heart attack; on her calendar "in tiny, controlled letters she wrote, 'All day it snowed' " (220). Borrowed words to lay against the silence. Herman Schultz: " 'Aw bug off. All of you cocksuckers'. . . . When his mother reached out and touched his golden head, he said, aw, bug off" (241). Language as tie that binds; language as knife that severs. In "The Day My Grandfather Died," adolescent Lureen parasitizes Claudette: "I had even picked up her accent and went out of my way to say things such as, 'The car, she is parked in the driveway,' and, 'H'it's going to rain' " (127). Lureen, in a voice not her own, attempts to speak, however exaggeratedly, her connection with her father's French blood. And Maurice himself has contributed to the (cultural and linguistic) silence that envelops Lureen: "How to be French, I didn't know. My father was seldom home and when he was, showed no interest or energy, I didn't know which, in perpetuating any of his own traditions" (131). Lureen senses that "to be like the Lafrenieres, my father's people, would make my rebellion complete and finally take me out and away from the rest of the family" (128), a separation she desires—"Being Mennonite was like having acne. It was shameful, dreary" (131)—but which, she comes to realize, has its own cost in isolation. Speaking with forked tongue.

Lureen has a perfect teacher in her father: Maurice, to fulfil his role as a responsible businessman/citizen, has traded in his own language and voice. His speech is peppered with clichés: " 'Howdy Doody' " (19), " 'You betcha' " (20), " 'Fancy meeting you here' " (144), "Not only do carrots give you good eyesight, they also give you hair on your chest. Look at me, Maurice said, living proof. Swallow a fruit pit and a tree will grow inside, bee stings are really smooches for sweet children" (36). Language as a dodge. When Betty, young and pregnant and angry, releases him from responsibility for her—" 'I'll be okay now. It's just been hard to adjust' " (119)—"Maurice brightens. He looks at her with a wide smile, his eyes uneasy though, carefully avoiding looking at her stomach. 'Adjust, absolutely. I can understand that. Certainly it takes time to get used to new situations' " (119). Language of smooth surfaces; language without challenge; language of diplomacy. Maurice speaks not in his own voice, but in "the quiet reasonable voice of Henry Roy, his mentor. He hoped it was the voice of someone who would listen for so long to the clamour of others and then, with a few chosen words, bring clarity to their ramblings so as to make them look ridiculous" (13). What survives of his communicative impulse is severely edited: "He saw himself begin to gesture expansively, his hand extended, palm up in a sweeping motion. . . . He dropped his arm quickly" (7). His reluctance to claim his own heritage, his need to be someone he is not—"to be agreeable and to keep the peace with all around him at any cost" (6)—cripples him, cripples his children too. A self-made man, a pastiche of others' surfaces: "Phrases, sentences, words that he'd picked out of the air all these years, formed by others. He had used them over and over without really knowing in what context they'd been said. He'd used words to build an image, not to express himself" (155). Adopting an assumed voice and language allows him tenuous access to his community but estranges him from his own individual and cultural voice; choosing to speak others' language wraps him in silence and sadness.

Betty, too, speaks borrowed words, but she seems more conscious of both cause and cost than either Maurice or Lureen. As she gathers her nerve to face the egg man in "The Wednesday Circle," verses from the Bible "rise unbidden" (47) to reassure her, to fortify her: " 'Lo, I am with you always even unto the end of the world,' her mind recites" (47); " 'Be not afraid,' a verse leaps into her head. 'For I am with you' " (49). Curiously, Betty is not absorbed by the Christian narrative so much as she absorbs it and revises it; she is drawn more to the group of women who represent it for her—her own growing sense of female community—than to the tenets of the faith. "The promise of their womanly strength is like a lamp unto her feet" (52). From her mouth: the language of the Bible in new contexts, in new configurations. From her mouth also: words that cry to be spoken, even when they are not her own. She reassures Herman's mother after a disastrous birthday party, "putting salve on hurt feelings" (242); she reassures her years later too, consciously concealing what the woman could not endure knowing. Language as gesture, a hand stretched across the silence. Betty speaking words that are hers and not hers:

> I remember my mother standing over my sick-bed after the doctor had left. She had scrubbed and rearranged the room before she'd called for him. Stripped the bed and put on the best linen. Well? she asked, her voice sharp in my fever-wracked head. Did he notice the pillow slips? Through the eyes of my sickness she appeared before me wavery and translucent. He asked me who did the wonderful needlework, I heard myself say, the words sluggish on my thick tongue. He liked the roses on the border. (242-43)

Much of oneself is lost or at least compromised in speaking in a borrowed voice. Even Betty's words, compassionate, sensitive to the other's need, form a one-way bridge; she reaches across the gap to comfort, but is herself then enveloped in silence, circumscribed by needs and fears she cannot speak. Betty and the other characters in this collection are propelled by desire, by yearning for contact, for connection, for escape from the margin. Maurice's insistence on being in the flooded town—"he couldn't explain to [Mika] that for once he didn't want to be on the outside, left out, but dead centre" (9)—finds echoes in other characters' determination to reach out of their silence, away from the margin, to establish connection. Tenuous contact. Sometimes intimacy. Bobbie, dreaming a life of romance, dreaming of Jeannie, struggles to accommodate her husband into her dream: "Wayne is a boring person. But she wants him to be interested in her. And so first she has to be interested in him, the book says" (288). Bobbie and Wayne, finally laughing over their defeats, bodies joining in their own pleasure. Mika, reaching out to another outsider, meeting him with her body, easing her isolation, her anger. Recognizing, too, their tacit boundaries: she a married woman, and James wanting only "a fleeting small part" (89) of her:

> he'd find her [hair] pins and he'd think of her for one second. She knew he wouldn't think of her longer than that, or wonder what she might be doing at that moment or try and recall her features as she did his; she even longed for the sight of his lanky body, his brown trousers flapping loosely about his ankles, the funny way he walked, arms swinging, leading with his ugly nose. I thought of you today, he'd said once. And I got this enormous stiff prick. I think of you too. She couldn't say, I love you. (86)

Affection, connection. And Lureen, young and angry, desperate about a world out of control, almost accidentally attaches herself to Larry. He teaches her the intricacies of the "eternal combustion engine" (208) and together they make love "every single day for six months" (204). Facing the void of his absence, she realizes "That I am in love with Larry. While waiting for the world to end, I have fallen in love. I fell for Larry Cooper. I'm falling" (213). The miraculous power of connection, physical and emotional, to counteract anger, desperation, hopelessness, to ease, perhaps momentarily to erase, the vacuum of silence. Even sometimes the dream of intimacy—Elizabeth carrying in her mind, on her skin, memories and imaginings of Hank—offers refuge from utter paralysis, from suspension in an inescapable hiatus.

Contact need not be explicitly physical. Maurice enjoys a kind of camaraderie in his barbershop; he even earns a nickname, "Old Man River," and the grudging respect of the larger community for his efforts to prepare the town for the flood. But he never quite belongs, just as Lureen never quite belongs to the group of frustrated housewives—"they spring-cleaned, read, kept the kids quiet on Saturday mornings and stayed attractive" (301)—who are her neighbours, her community. And the Wednesday Circle, the women's study group to which Mika belongs, impresses Betty as united, protective, powerful:

> they're there in the dining room, sitting in a circle with their Bibles in their laps. It's like women and children in the centre. And arrows flying. Wagons are going up in flames and smoke. The goodness and matronly wisdom of the Wednesday Circle is a newly discovered thing. She belongs with them now. They can reach out to protect her even here, by just being what they are. (46)

The Wednesday Circle is not, as Betty discovers, united, protective, powerful. It can survive as a community only by censoring certain attitudes, by relegating particular people, particular ideas to silence on the margins. By imposing silence. But it also allows, simply by existing, for the occasional sharing of a truer (unedited) experience of the world: Mika admitting to thoughts of suicide, met by dismay, by intimidation. Met also by compassion, by recognition of her courage. Tenuous connection. Contact.

For most of these characters, community is not so much the loose groupings of people who profess similar ideas or who are thrown together by virtue of proximity; for them, community is embodied in the complex interrelations that comprise family. Sisters and brothers, parents and children and children's children. Lines of blood, blood relations. Complex connections. Tenuous contact by pen, "confession . . . through a sheet of paper, as if through the lace-like grating of the confessional" (Manguel 14): Lureen's children struggle to support one another and to establish a relationship with their mother; Lureen earlier, a young mother, longing for contact, thinks of her own mother, "That I should write her a letter. But I didn't know what I would say" (274). Family relations. And contact through special treasures: Elizabeth drinks from a china cup brought from Russia by her mother, passed from mother to daughter; Mika recovers from storage Betty's severed childhood braids; unsentimental Lureen sorts and then repacks "booties and bonnets, . . . burp-stained nighties, yellow, white and green" (253); Betty sends her children out into the world with "surprises to be . . . unpack[ed]" (159) from their trunks, reminders of home. Connections of custom: Lureen, worried about building a family without customs, isolated especially at Easter from her own family, connected, too, by perfect memory of their shared rituals:

> She missed the smell of the bread baking, the toadstool-shaped loaves crawling up and out of their cans and collars of wax paper. She missed the Easter baskets. Her sisters took turns making them, decorating them in mustard yellow and purple crepe paper. Even now, her mother was probably rolling coloured eggs across newspapers to dry and planning Easter baskets for the youngest ones still at home and for the grandchildren who would be there for Sunday dinner. (297)

Complicated mazes of family connections. Lureen: a Cooper, a Lafreniere, a Thiessen, claiming and disclaiming alliance, always and invariably belonging, built into the (family) body, disallowed the margin. Lureen grieving finally, despite her determination to be French, for the deep love and profound impact of an old Mennonite man: " 'An old man is an old man, right? It doesn't matter what nationality, they're all the same. He was old and he was mine and he died' " (141). And Maurice, ultimately reclaimed by the heritage he refused to admit; dying, he recovers his mother's moccasin, meets Old Man Desmarais, and hears the irresistible call of the blue heron:

> He turned and saw them, hundreds, rising from the water, necks pulled in tightly, iridescent beads dropping from their blue wings. . . . Maurice reached, caught hold of a scaly, rough bird leg. Blue wings fanned about his head, struggled against his weight. . . . It faltered, climbed, and then he was skimming across the top of the water, weightless, free, upstream on the river, through its loops and curls out, out to the broad mouth

> where the colour of the water beneath him changed and the muddy silt settled to the bottom and there stretched before him the endless blue of the giant lake. (157)

Bonds of memory. Memory: perhaps even "the source of truth in these stories—memory because it determines reality by creating the past on which the real world stands" (Manguel 15). Maurice's remembrance of his parents, his ancestors; Mika's incantation about her children:

> I had one who used to walk off chairs. . . . I had one who ate dirt. . . . I had one who hated water. . . . I had one who, one day, came home from school or from wherever she had been. . . . And who, for no reason I know of, marched upstairs into my bedroom and took the scissors from the sewing box and cut off her hair. . . . I had one who played the most beautiful music. . . . I had one who ate chalk. No, it wasn't chalk. It was dirt. I had one who ate rat poison. . . . I had one who used to loosen the caps on my pear preserves so the syrup would ferment. (344-53)

Bonds of memory, bonds of belonging. Overwhelming the division, separation, isolation. Silencing the silencing.

Yet another escape from the margin: to place oneself in the middle of the maze, to learn to listen to, to refuse to silence, one's own voice. Connection with the world through connection with oneself. Shifting the parameters. Elizabeth peels away layers of reserve, assuming both the challenge and power of decision-making: "I plan to sell, she'd said, as though it was her farm to sell. And saying it made it seem real" (234). Assuming also the challenge and power of living her own life, taking into account not only the needs of son and husband, but also the needs—financial, emotional, sexual—of her self. Freed into life: "She would go to see the falls. She would hold onto the railing or she would let herself go. Whatever she did, she would do willingly" (236). And Truda, facing absolute solitude and silence on Toronto Street, stepping out of the girdle that binds her flesh into a shape acceptable to the world, coming to recognize her painfully constricted self: afraid of the dark, fearful of losing her way, ashamed of her preoccupation with food, disgusted with the cautiousness of her public image, terrified of being alone. She discovers also that where she had felt most safe—in her marriage to Brian—she had been most severely silenced:

> she'd suddenly realized that they would never have children. He never intended they would. All this waiting to build the house and a patio, to take the vacations had been a lie. She couldn't forgive him, not for that. During their perfect vacation, the second honeymoon, standing in her queen-sized bathing suit, she was quietly sorrowful, listening to something inside herself cracking open, a sluggish, deadening feeling creeping into its place. (313-14)

Truda, taking her life into her own hands, moving out of the gap into a new kind of silence. A silence of potential: a space to hear herself, a space to speak herself.

Listening to—and trusting—one's own voice is particularly crucial for the artist, and several of Birdsell's characters are artists. Betty responds instinctively to Mrs. Schultz' music: "I listened, my mouth suddenly stiff and shaking. The music was not a lullaby, but something else that made me stand still, my breasts leaning into it. My fingers began moving on their own across the table top, tracing the graceful cadences, the rising and falling of it" (244); she learns, herself, to play the piano, and as an adult shares her gift, teaching others to play too. Lureen incorporates her fascination with her own ancestry and her struggle to survive into heritage boxes, planning one shaped like a house, "But instead of squares for photographs and family momentoes, I would have eyes in the box, different shapes, colours, staring out through the glass" (339). And Truda, drawing by the hour as a child, salves the pain of abandonment and fear: "crying made everything worse. But she'd discovered that crayons and paper made it better. Drawing was a bird moving against a clean sky the way you wanted it to" (43). Truda, who sees incomparable beauty in a young girl-bride wrapped in a sheet and wearing a lace curtain veil, who sees in spite of, rather than because of, the elaborate narrative of romance that envelops weddings and the equally powerful narrative of social stratification that circumscribes the girl's family. Eyes of an artist. Perceiving the world through thick lenses, translating it back to itself in drawings, in pots. Expressing her world, expressing her connection with that world. Speaking into the gap; speaking out of the gap.

Birdsell's stories pulse with fear, with desperation, with anger. They refuse to shy away from the turmoil of the working-class world, from the silencing of those on the margin. They suggest the so-called "dirty realism" of Raymond Carver, Ann Beattie, Bobbie Ann Mason, and other anti-epiphanic chroniclers of the working class, but Birdsell cleaves to another aesthetic, one that entertains possibilities, however muted, of progress, of improvement: Mika's children are able to stray away from the stifling support systems—religious, moral, social, sexual narratives—that her parents would not have been without; they are (apparently) more honest with themselves, with their partners, with their children. Muted possibilities for improvement. Necessarily muted: these stories determinedly root themselves in the world, refusing the notion of transcendence. In the world, of the world. Imagining into existence some new reality, a utopia, is not Birdsell's interest; and whereas reconfiguring extant material, the game of the bricoleur, cannot recreate the world, it can transform a margin into a space. Space to breathe, space to speak.

William New suggests that Canadian short story writers can be distinguished roughly by whether they "ultimately redirect their readers' attention back to the world . . . or to the sheer artifice of their own arrangements of verbal and visual signs" (106); Birdsell he places in the latter group. I think not. Her stories seem to me rather to insist on the reality (and even the perfectibility) of the world to which they refer (McCormack 20-21). Staunch realism. With a touch of wistfulness. But without that sinewy power that accompanies an acute awareness of the difficulties and dangers of attempting to bridge the chasm, the gap, the silence, between world and word. Birdsell points so resolutely that she ends up erasing the language with which she points. Obscuring much of what she would like to say. Silencing herself. "Fiction," Geoff Hancock argues, "tells us stories about stories" (289). Birdsell resists that pull from story to fiction. She tells stories, fine stories. She does not quite create fictions.

Works Cited

Birdsell, Sandra. *Agassiz Stories*. Winnipeg: Turnstone Press, 1987.

Foster, Hal. *Recodings: Art, Spectacle, Cultural Politics*. Seattle: Bay Press, 1985.

Hancock, Geoff. "Moving off the Map: from 'Story' to 'Fiction'." *Canadian Fiction Magazine* 50-51 (1984): 277-90.

Laurence, Margaret. *A Bird in the House*. Toronto: McClelland and Stewart, 1970.

Levi-Strauss, Claude. *The Savage Mind*. London: Weidenfeld & Nicolson, 1966.

Manguel, Alberto. "Everything under the Sun." Review of *Ladies of the House*. *Books in Canada* 14.1 (1985): 14-16.

McCormack, Eric. "A Conversation with Sandra Birdsell." *The New Quarterly* 8.2 (1988): 9-22.

Munro, Alice. *Lives of Girls and Women*. Toronto: McGraw-Hill Ryerson, 1971.

New, William. *Dreams of Speech and Violence*. Toronto: University of Toronto Press, 1987.

Spalding, Linda. "The Ripple Effect." Review of *Night Travellers* and *Ladies of the House*. *Canadian Forum* 65 (1985): 28-29.

Figures on a Wharf: Shaping Things to Come

Birk Sproxton

Wayne Tefs has been on a quiet campaign over the past decade. In his stories, reviews and essays, in his work as editor and compiler of fiction, and in three novels he has carried on an assault against entrenched notions about prairie writing. His primary target has been the mindset which assumes that prairie writing is necessarily concerned with rural people dominated by the landscape. As a novelist, Tefs sets his second novel, *The Cartier Street Contract*, an urban political drama in a realist mode, in Montreal during the October Crisis; and he sets his third novel, *The Canasta Players*, primarily in Winnipeg. As a critic, Tefs identifies "the hayseed factor" as a reason why writers like Robert Kroetsch and David Arnason, for example, do not enjoy the attention accorded to more traditional writers like W.O. Mitchell and Sandra Birdsell. While he recognizes and appreciates the importance of the realist tradition—and celebrates in particular the very fine work of Birdsell—he argues for the importance of writing which challenges readers' expectations about what writing is.

In his column in *Border Crossings* Tefs writes of Manitoba short stories, British novels and Australian novels.[1] He campaigns to enlarge the field, to make room for new forms and techniques, new visions and ideas.

In a 1985 essay Tefs brings some of these concerns together in a nuanced and subtle way. "Current Prairie Fiction: Openings/Beginnings" argues that Robert Kroetsch has moved prairie fiction into a new ethos. Tefs puts it this way:

> With Kroetsch the prairie novel begins to transform the landscape rather than to be moulded by it. . . . Where in the typical early prairie novel landscape dominated people, it is now shaped by the (usually erotic and irreverent) human imagination. ("Current," *Trace* 246-47)

This change involves more than a matter of technique; it amounts in fact to a new vision, and this new vision often appears in the very openings of the novels. The chief element in the new way of seeing, Tefs argues, assumes the importance of play, as in *What the Crow Said*, for example, which opens with the seduction of Vera Lang by a swarm of bees. As a consequence of this new way of seeing, where we once had irony we now have the comic; where we once had the defeated shrug we now have laughter. "Ridicule replaces angst, sympathy [replaces] oppression, and sexual energy, helplessness" ("Current," *Trace* 247). Prairie novelists, Tefs concludes, are on the cusp of a new development which moves "away from the ironic vision of the realistic landscape novel toward a more triumphant human perspective . . ." (248). Even so—and he may well be too optimistic in his assessment of current directions—the argument needs to be made again and again, for some readers and some critics habitually think of the novel as a realistic thing, and old habits prove hard to break.

---

1 See Tefs' essays in *Border Crossings*: "The Aussies: From Outback to Paperback"; "Travels with Mrs. Torture"; "The Hayseed Factor in Prairie Fiction."

Some of the habits appear in the responses to Tefs' *Figures on a Wharf*. Nominated for the *Books in Canada* Best First Novel Award upon its publication in 1983, *Figures* received critical praise in reviews across the country for its powerful treatment of a love triangle. In a series of dated chapters covering the period of about one year, the narrative centres on a university professor named Michael, who finds himself torn between a dutiful attachment to his wife, Patricia, and the affections of a (married) graduate student, Mary. Many readers have praised the handling of the female characters, particularly Patricia. The characters are praised for the solidity they manifest: they give the illusion of being historical people, in the tradition of realist fiction.

Praise has not been unanimous, though. Some readers have been puzzled by the structure of the novel, more specifically by the function of brief first-person sections placed between the longer third-person chapters. How do these interchapters work? Why does Tefs avoid a linear structure in the sequence of the dated chapters? What does his title mean?

These and other questions about the novel can be addressed by considering *Figures* in the light of the essay on openings. Tefs in *Figures* deliberately plays with the conventions and expectations of the realist tradition, and much of the novel's energy derives from its opposition to the so-called hayseed factor. *Figures* challenges the clichéd and persistent notion of prairie fictions as unsophisticated re-runs of the familiar landscape motif. The novel gives us urban and urbane men and women, two (or three?) distinct yet related lines of narrative, and a narrator who speaks in two voices. Instead of a beginning, middle, and end, it offers us beginnings and endings, and lets them take care of the middles. The title, moreover, alluding as it does to a painting in the mode of magic realism, alerts us to the possibility that we must deal with more than a traditional realistic landscape novel.

Beginnings/Opening

1.

To begin with the epigraphs. The first, from the Latin poet Propertius, stresses the power of love and its ineluctable doubleness: "love alone loves no physician of its ill." Love: a tangle of emotions, perhaps incurable, perhaps idiopathic, certainly perverse. The many facets of love comprise the subject of the novel. As Michael puts it in a review referred to in the text, the modern novelist has failed to acknowledge the capacity in the human heart "to love two people at once, differently, but just as meaningfully and sincerely" (101). Whether or not Michael rationalizes here, and the text suggests that he does, *Figures* as a whole explores love as a plurality.

For a second epigraph, Tefs turns to George Meredith's sonnet sequence "Modern Love." Meredith's images in the quoted lines emphasize the tension between fluidity and stasis: "She lay / Stone-still, and the long darkness flowed away / With muffled pulses." These images, or variations on them, as we shall see, inform the novel. The last lines of the Meredith quotation emphasize the paralysis of the lovers described as "moveless" from "head to feet . . . ," lovers overwhelmed with a sense of loss as they look "through their dead black years, / By vain regret scrawled over the blank wall." Together the two quotations indicate an elegiac tone, which prefigures one quality of the novel's mood, though not necessarily the dominant one, for the narrative proves more forward-looking than the epigraphs suggest.

2.

One narrative begins on the first page with an undated and unnumbered chapter in the third person. "Among these photographs," it begins, establishing the narrator as a researcher cum biographer, "Among these photographs there is one of Michael's family . . ." (1). This chapter focuses on one particular photograph, just as the last chapter of the book does. Together these two comprise a frame for the novel: the narrative therefore is delivered from some time later than the "Summer 1980" written across the photo, the subject of the end chapter. We conclude that the pages between the frame chapters constitute an extended flashback of the time between "August 1978," the date on the first photograph selected, and the summer of 1980. As we see, however, the middle chapters all fall into the period February 15, 1979 to September 21, 1979. Not seamless and continuous, the narrative gives us glimpses only, fragments, pieces of things.

This first frame chapter puts Michael and his family on centre stage, as it were, figures caught in time. Michael's eyes are "focused into distance," they look "fixed" (2). Patricia for her part wears a mask for the camera. As our narrator puts it, "she set her face to smile through the summers . . ." (3). Held up for scrutiny in this way, Michael and Patricia are more figures than characters: flat, two-dimensional, static.

This chapter foregrounds the narrator as a "character" in the drama. He shows himself to be knowing. He knows the characters on a first-name basis (Michael, Patricia, Michael's friend and colleague, Stephen), he knows what happened the night before the photo was taken, how many snaps Stephen took to get one right. He knows what has been happening in the relationship between Michael and Patricia. Though the photo shows them to be for the moment physically close, the narrator speaks of the distance between them, how Patricia has grown to resent Michael's friends and his seeming refusal to spend time alone with her. He knows too, we presume, of the other photos, the ones not spoken of here directly but which inform his vision. He addresses the reader as a friend of the principal characters, concerned yet objective. As readers we become lookers-on, voyeurs who overhear the inside story—a familiar situation for readers of realist fiction.

3.

The narrator's attitude toward Michael emerges partly in the immediately succeeding chapter. Here we begin again. The "chapter," very short, less than a page, is set in an italic face, which immediately marks it to be different from the other chapters. This play with the text's surface dislocates assumptions we might have about the novel's unity, because we clearly do not have a seamless monological narrative. Now Tefs uses a first-person point of view and his tone appears to be more casual. The narrator is no longer simply the knowing reporter who comments on both the outer and inner lives of the characters. Now the narrator reveals himself even as he speaks of Michael. This chapter, or better, this interchapter, parallels a similar interchapter placed as the penultimate unit of the novel. These two units (5, 229) therefore form a second frame, an inner frame to the opening and closing sections on photographs (1-3, 230). Both of these interchapters begin, "Michael says . . ." (5, 229). The narrator, Boswell-like, records and comments on Michael's *obiter dicta*. The effect doubles the narrative. We now begin to respond both to the narrator and to his narrative.

4.

Other openings include the chronological beginning, dated "February 15, 1979"; the July "exchange" between Mary and Michael, which marks a new beginning for them; the September 21 scene, which sees Michael leaving Patricia, and Patricia turning back into the house to start her life again. These many beginnings both truncate the linearity of the narrative and layer it. Tefs thus dispenses with the transparent narrative which a more traditional realism aims for. We become aware of the composition, experience the novel as a made thing. The story-teller's voice in those little chapters reminds us that we are being given a story: "Michael says," or "What you don't know is this." These little stories help us see the big narrative as a story too, and to realize our part in it. It's as if the narrator says, "Look at these photos, consider this possibility," and out of such fragments the reader must construct a tale. Our situation becomes analogous to the reader of Findley's *The Wars*. We are given the bits and pieces, and must participate by putting them together. Perhaps, as Findley has it, "the corner of a picture will reveal the whole" (10-11). In any case, that is all we have; some say that is all we ever have.

Structure

This deceptively simple device of the interchapters has large implications for the narrative. They become themselves another textual thread. They interrupt the narrative development, give another voice to the novel, provide a reference point or index to the unfolding drama of Michael-Patricia-Mary. In this way, Michael and his loves are set in relief, foregrounded against the background of the narrator's own experiences with love. The small events the interchapters present—each of them a little scene—parallel, contrast, or extend the events of the larger narrative.

Voice

The interchapters add another voice to the text and show the narrator commenting on his own values and attitudes. In this way Tefs plays with the traditional realist convention that has the narrator aloof as a transcendental God. By contrast, the human narrator in *Figures* identifies himself, even tells us a confidential tale or two about his own weaknesses and foibles, and thus places the writer himself at one more remove from the text. Tefs insists in this way that the narrator is a central part of the fiction, whether he be the seemingly anonymous, objective, distanced voice of the larger narrative, or the casual, almost chummy voice of the interchapters. The narrator therefore both tells what he knows of the love triangle, and also reads his own telling. "That reminds me . . . ," begins one of the interchapters (141). Readers of the novel thus become involved twice over: once as readers of the Michael biography, and again as the confidantes of the first-person narrator of the interchapters. "You remember . . . ," he says (93), or "I've never told anyone before" (77), or "What you don't know is this" (17). The narrator as biographer, researcher and archivist tells us of Michael's love life, and also of his own love life, or at least parts of it. When he says, "That reminds me," we anticipate his story of Joan (the subject of an interchapter on page 29) and Anna (67). His voice in the interchapters takes us into another register as he assumes the role of a beer parlour story-teller. His language, informal, earthy, colloquial, at times obscene, reveals more passion than that of the archivist-biographer.

The narrator's attitudes towards Michael change over the course of the narrative. Both the framing interchapters show Michael as a story-teller, the person at the centre of the group. But a subtle change takes place in the narrator from the first of these to the last, a change that alerts us to the nuances of the final photo chapter. In the first interchapter, Michael asserts to his male audience that men on their death beds always think of the "tail they've missed" (5). The group around him has been "eager to hear"; the narrator himself assents to Michael's opinion, though he's reluctant to agree ("Shit, he's right again"). Here the narrator defers to Michael's views, but the interchapter which closes the frame shows Michael to be less assertive, less confident because shaded with the narrator's scepticism. Michael again speaks in his aphoristic mode, and again to an exclusively male audience. This time he says he believes women will always "be there" for men, they will always be there "to mother us" (229). Yet even as he relates Michael's speech, the narrator shows reserve. The first hint of distance between Michael and the narrator appears in the opening of the sentence, "I've heard him say this before. . . ." The doubtfulness becomes more apparent as the sentence moves to its close: "but now, seeing the almost imperceptible twitch that punctuates his jaw before he quickly inhales on his cigarette, I wonder if even he believes it." This sentence, the last of the last interchapter, leaves the matter neatly unresolved, an open question.

Parallels

These interchapters also parallel the unfolding drama among Patricia, Michael, and Mary. For example, in the second interchapter the narrator speaks of the physical pleasure of an embrace and then hints at the inevitable decay of the woman's body and his determination to hang on to the memory of that special moment with her. "I want only to remember Lou as she was on that day, auburn hair, mint breath" (17). He wishes to stop time, he desires stasis even as he is aware of the inevitability of change. In this respect his desires parallel those of Michael. The past has been good; therefore he wishes to hold on to it. At the same time, though, he has other desires. Holding on conflicts with letting go. In the immediately preceding scene Michael meets Mary in a parking lot, and they hold each other. Yet Michael is annoyed that Mary has called him away from what he wanted to do; he thinks she acts like a wife. He both wants her and doesn't want her. The narrator's position vis-a-vis Michael resembles a voice that Michael once heard in his dreams (before his desire for Mary made him restless): "Sometimes a narrator spoke like the voice-over in movie tracks, lending authenticity to his welter of sensations" (20). When he speaks in the first person, our narrator tells us of some of the vicissitudes of love that he has experienced, and thereby puts Michael and his story in a familiar context.

Contrast

At other times the relationship is one of contrast. The most dramatic occurs between the "July 1979" chapter and the subsequent interchapter. The July chapter consists of two modes and two voices: (1) letters from Mary (on vacation in British Columbia) to Michael (in Winnipeg); and (2) Michael's imaginary responses to her. The two modes in fact are two variations of the basic strategy of the love lyric: an apostrophe to the absent loved one. The chapter does not quite become lyrical, but it makes the main point: that these two people are in love (and therefore somewhat foolish in the "private" communications we are privileged to overhear). Then comes the contrast. In the interchapter our narrator tells of a bragging bully who has forced a woman to have sex with him in a boat. The narrator's disgust for this bully contrasts sharply with the rhapsodic conceits of the lovers, and provides an abrupt reminder of the complexities of man-woman relations.

Extension

In other instances the interchapters extend the motifs of the main narrative. The most important of these extensions in terms of both the plot and the narrator's attitude toward the Michael-Mary-Patricia love triangle occurs late in the text when Patricia arrives at the lake to confront Michael about his taking Mary to the cottage. At this point in the novel, Tefs has begun to concentrate his narrative by focusing on the events of mid-June. The earlier chapters, the ones closer to the front of the book, generalize ("March 1979," "April 1979," "July 1979") or represent slices of time ("April 1," "May 1," "February 15," "March 21"). The former chapters stress mood, tend to be reflective, expository, more diegetic than mimetic. The latter are detailed, dense takes, with emphasis upon action and time, the present moment, what has happened, what may happen, mimetic. The confrontation episode fits in the mimetic strand. It covers two chapters, the only event dealt with in such detail. The date is 21 June. Tefs has carefully built up to this point by a sequence of chapters treated in chronological order—June 12, June 13, June 15, June 17. The strategy seeks to gain power by accumulation.

The first of the 21 June chapters brings out Patricia's pain and anger. She shouts and begins to throw dishes and bottles to the floor in her rage. The last two paragraphs emphasize her screams and Michael's helplessness:

> "Don't, Patricia," he pleads, but to himself, for he can see she doesn't hear, is following the track of her own thoughts only. He backs into the table, cutting his foot on a shard of glass. Blood mixes with the remains of Patricia's drink and translucent scarlet smears the linoleum.
>
> "Michael," Patricia screams as she lunges out of the bedroom toward him. The sound is so shrill one latticed kitchen window trembles with vibrations. "Michael," she screams again. She stumbles over the woven carpet where it is crushed against the sofa. The sound is so shrill Michael's mind goes blank. (210)

The ending leaves in suspense exactly what happens, but the interchapter provides a clue: "Only once a girl ever hit me," our narrator begins. He goes on to conclude that while he first thought the girl's act "cowardly"—she hit him at "an unguarded moment"—he later concluded that "she was right. Against the tongue lashers of the world brute physical acts are the only response" (211). At this juncture the two texts stand poised against each other. We may be ready to condemn Patricia for her violence (at the beginning of the next chapter we learn she has seized a butcher knife and raised it above her shoulder to attack Michael) but the narrator's anecdote gives us pause. Yes, we might say, a physical response to emotional pain is appropriate. And yet . . .

Images/Figures

Begin again. The first dated chapter, "March 21, 1979," focuses on a phone call from Mary to Michael which ironically places him again on the receiving end of a woman's actions, as he is in the chronological beginning (one more parallel). In this March beginning he is "drifting" in reverie, afloat in time, when Mary calls:

> When the phone rang Michael was months distant, drifting in sand and sea. Though it was March, the end of term weeks away, examinations and final papers still ahead, his eyes, clouded by gin, rolled over memories of beaches, waves pounding rocks and wooden docks. The way, near shore, water boiled back upon itself murky brown; or farther out, emerald green, and blue, tossed and frothed in summer winds. Once he'd sailed on a perfect August day, pounding waves beating a subliminal tune on the hull, spelling away other sounds. An endless silence prolonged such summer afternoons with their blue skies, when waves cast knives of sun so jagged they cut the eye. The kind of air and sun that drove you home exhausted, that propelled expended limbs and nerves to that great darkness, oblivion. (7)

The images here of water and states of consciousness echo the fluid images of the epigraphs and prefigure the natural, man-made, and bodily fluids of the novel. "Drifting" thoughts and memories "clouded by gin," "subliminal" tunes, water "boiled" and "tossed and frothed," the "darkness" of "oblivion," all these contend with the jagged knives (another ironic prefiguring) of the sun. This is a world of early summer romance, a world coming into the fullness of being.

The novel is literally awash in water (the shiftiest of the four classic elements) and other liquids. The crucial scenes between Michael and Mary and Michael and Patricia take place at Lake Winnipeg; many of the narrator's love adventures occur at Clear Lake (Diamond Lake in the Margaret Laurence Manawaka fiction). Michael, the novel's prime drifter, thinks how he and Patricia "had drifted into marriage and now, it seemed to him, they were drifting out of it" (88). In an expansive party mood, Michael sucks on his liquor and cigarettes while extolling the values of D.H. Lawrence, especially his glorification of sex: "Man . . . bathes in its curative waters," he says (37). Patricia, in a more domestic scene, wakes suddenly from a nightmare to find Michael standing beside her with a glass of water (151). In another fantasy, Patricia imagines herself smashing Michael's head and the spurting out of his blood (138). Our narrator finds himself, after a moment of unconsummated passion, lying flat on a pier "listening to waves shushing up the sand" (29). All the characters, in both narratives, consume vast quantities of beer, scotch, gin, rye, rum, champagne.

In one of the Lake Winnipeg scenes, Tefs explicitly links love and fluency. Michael catches his finger, specifically his wedding ring, on a loose piece of arborite in his cabin and cuts himself. (Later, Patricia catches one of her rings on a counter in their house [138]. A telling parallelism.) He walks down to the lake sucking his finger, tasting blood mingled with the rye he has been drinking. He dips his hand into the ice-cold water of early April and reflects upon the restlessness of the lake.

> Wave followed wave, no two ever identical, yet all conforming to a basic, elusive pattern. Movement. Fluidity of matter. Love, he thought, is a fluid emotion, running pell-mell up this break, driven by intense forces, crashing down over there, trickling to a stream and even stopping, sometimes pooling, inert. And monogamy a vessel trying to contain swirling movement. One elastic, the other inelastic. Forged together by smithies of what human need? Security? Dependability? Fear? (100)

Inertia against movement, the basic configuration of the images. By extension marriage is inelastic, a containing (restraining?) vessel. Here Michael's imagination shapes the landscape, lakescape. The lake does not overwhelm him; rather he sees in its movements the shape of his own needs and desires. A comment later by Mary in one of her letters sheds light on Michael's reflections at the water's edge. She says that he is narcissistic, not an ego-maniac (158). Narcissus, the one who upon looking into the water fell in love with his own image.

Tefs often uses water images to define some aspect of his characters' inner lives, following the William Jamesian convention which figures consciousness as a stream. In March, when he has not yet been forced into making decisions about his life, still attached to Patricia and his family and drawn to Mary, and adrift in the middle, Michael dreams in water images: "He seemed to drift into a pellucid world of images that floated tantalizingly and then vaporized before he could lay hold of them, mold them to his desire" (20). He later moulds the waves at the beach into reflections on the nature of marriage, monogamy as a vessel trying to contain an emotion as powerful and fluid as a huge lake.

In the knife scene, Tefs moves close to the filmic device of slow motion when he describes Patricia moving as if in water. "Moe yelled from the door, *Patricia*, *Patricia*, and she turned like a diver under water, slowly, her body distended, and her thoughts drifted like bubbles away from Michael" (213-14). The cabin is splattered with broken glass, spilled drinks, spilled blood. Later in the same scene, Michael, alone, realizes what has been happening: "*I could be dead*, he thought, *I could be dead*. His bowels liquified, but he could not raise his body. He was drowned in feeling and he slumped backward dizzily" (221). Love as a fluid emotion, body as a vessel. Interestingly, this last scene echoes a recognition scene from Charles Yale Harrison's *Generals Die in Bed* in which the unnamed narrator experiences the liquefaction of his bowels in the midst of an artillery attack. In *Generals*, a classic *Bildungsroman*, this moment of awakening occurs during the narrator's very first bombardment (24). In *Figures*, Tefs places this awakening near the end of the narrative, as if in the battles of love consciousness is delayed, resisted, hard to come by. Consciousness, death, feces, fluidity, end things.

Point of View

As the quotations and illustrations above will suggest, Tefs shifts centre of consciousness within and among the chapters that make up the larger narrative. In deftly handled shifts he takes us now inside Michael's head, now inside Patricia's, later inside Mary's. Consider again one sentence from the confrontation scene. It starts with Michael, speaking aloud: " 'Don't, Patricia,' he pleads, but to himself, for he can see she doesn't hear, is following the track of her own thoughts only" (210). The sentence moves quickly from a representation of speech, to a comment on Michael's awareness, and then to his sense of her awareness, the single-minded "track" that she rides so ominously.

Tefs also likes to report on the dreams and fantasies of his characters. This movement to the inner life from the outer and from one character to another creates a rhythm for the novel, another textual weave. We could review our list of beginnings, add to the list the first chapter which establishes Patricia as the centre of consciousness, "April 1, 1979." Is she the one who is being fooled? Add the first chapter in which Mary is centre of consciousness, "June 11, 1979." Until this point her inner life has been presented in more conventional indirect ways. She tells Michael why she got married in the first place, for instance. Or the narrator says "she thinks." Or Tefs has her write letters, another way to represent the inner private life of a character. Fluently.

Intertexts

The novel's intertextual links include those I have mentioned in passing (Laurence's Manawaka fiction, *The Wars*, *Generals Die in Bed*—why two war novels? Love as a battle?). And those named in the text proper, like Freud, F. Scott Fitzgerald, John Fowles, Hemingway, D.H. Lawrence, and so on. A subtext to *Figures* is an aesthetic that asserts the importance of bodily imperatives, a vision which attempts to give play to desire in all its manifestations. Hence the novelist takes cognizance of Leslie Fiedler's assertion, in *Love and Death in the American Novel*, that an essential difference between the American novel and the European arises from the former's "chary treatment of women and of sex" (31), and attempts to address that imbalance. (In the gallery scene with Mary, Michael, a latter-day Romantic, conjoins death and beauty in a comment on a painting: " 'Here . . . is what the prairie is all about. Beauty joined to energy. Light to dark. Life to death. People don't realize how deathly its beauty is; or rather how beautiful its death is' " [113].)

The title declares another important intertextual connection. This link intrigues because of its provocative ambiguity. The title does not fit the historical world the novel renders. Prairie people do not speak of wharfs; they speak rather, as the characters in the novel do, of piers or docks. The title has a defamiliarizing effect. *Figures on a Wharf* echoes the title of an Alex Colville painting, *Four Figures on a Wharf* (1952), an unusual work in the painter's *oeuvre*, enigmatic, perhaps symbolic in some personal way. Commentators on the painting speak of the work as autobiographical in origin, turning back to Colville's war years:

> *Four Figures on a Wharf* is an abstraction of memory, a reflection on Colville's desire to return home and be reunited with his wife. But by giving it a loosely classical ambience he suggests his concern is with the essence, not with the actual fact of "waiting." We cannot identify specific fears and longings in the women; they are anonymous even in the characterless drapery that they wear. We are turned back from them to the painting's viewpoint, as if we are standing on the shore, literally and figuratively standing back from events, creating an idealized image of memory. (Burnett 80)

An earlier commentator, Helen J. Dow, identifies the four figures as aspects of Colville's wife. Her view too, however, stresses the longing and the love that the painting manifests.

> It depicts four statuesque figures of a semi-nude woman, each one more draped than the last, as they move slowly down a long wharf jutting into a serene sea. The figures are seen from the back, as though they were waiting for a ship. All four appear to be the same person at a different moment, obviously the artist's wife as she moves gracefully toward the long-expected ship which, though unseen, presumably draws near in the distance. As the form changes from nude to draped, perhaps it represents first the anticipation simply of woman in general, and then specifically of this woman, the artist's wife; for the painting is a love-lyric commemorating the joy of reunion. (59-62)

The wharf becomes a kind of stage, and the figure as she moves away and draws into her draping becomes more enigmatic. The figure at the end of the wharf, though her arms are not in the motion of removing her robe as are the other figures, seems more fully poised to become active, for she stands very near the stark vertical line marking the edge of the wharf. Movement and stasis held in tension.

What connects the painting and the novel? At one level the novel's title alerts us to a challenge of the visual sense. The text explicitly invites us to overhear the narrator speak about photographs, and within the third-person narrative we encounter a lexicon which ranges from the art image to the photographic image to the filmic image. In a gallery scene, for example, Michael starts to lecture Mary on the meaning of an oil painting which shows a prairie sky fractured by lightning. Later, in the same episode, after they have made love, Mary reluctantly responds to Michael's need to talk. "She wants to lay there," we learn, "and tread the sensation, the way you come out of a film sometimes, not wanting to talk about it" (116). A few minutes later while they drink champagne and reminisce, they recollect how earlier they agreed that they would allow love to take them where it would, to expose themselves: "Not only to people, but to time. A kind of double exposure" (118). In a general way, the novelist explores different kinds and levels of visualization, or exploits our awareness of these levels and our ability to recognize movement from one to another. Photos are figures frozen in time, like the frozen figures of the Colville painting. We find in such freezing of time an echo of the epigraph from George Meredith's "Modern Love": ". . . they from head to feet / Were moveless. . . . " The title, in referring to an art image, represents one level of abstraction beyond the photo image. Not the carpenter's table, but the idea of a table. The title challenges us to see the novel not as realism, but as art, a thing composed, like a painting.

Connections between the painting and the novel. Some other possibilities:

Love, separation, homecoming. A sea voyage / see voyage. Reader as voyeur, *mon semblable*, *ma soeur*.

Waiting. Penelope waiting. Her disguises, masks. Waiting and wanting. Green and white. Jealousy? Fear?

The art image, draping and undraping. Lapping of waves, the solidity of the wharf. Floating. A figure foregrounded, four times.

The cold shoulder.

Absence. What you do not see is what there was / is. The presence of an absence. The (assumed) solidity of the shoreline, an anchorage point, fixed for seeing. There was / there is:

a face (a wharf, a war)
a woman / a man
face to face
(an undraping)
eye to eye
warm hands
war members

> war(m) embers
> (war)m embrace
> m m m m m m

> Michael's arm disappears behind Mary's back, and his fingers can be seen resting along the folds of her sweater, the other side of her waist. They have been walking. . . . It may be only the way this evening light splashes across her breasts and waist, but she seems to have gained weight. She is half-looking at Michael as if they are sharing a joke, and the lines around her eyes and mouth are relaxed and make her girlish. . . . His smile is full and relaxed; fingers of pleasure race up one cheek. (231)

Closings

But. A good novel always has a but, a contradiction, a tension. The novel does not close here. E.M. Forster, speaking of last things, says that a deadness in endings is the inherent weakness of the novel as a form (102-03). But in *Figures* we have the hint of new things to come. A multiple ending.

An ending, with Patricia:

> As the engine started, Patricia turned away, hugging arms around her body for warmth, and walked quickly up the sidewalk to the front door, looking straight ahead, focused already on the dim interior of her own house and the effort of putting it in order. (227)

No Odysseus here. She is focused, and she will put her house in order.

Or another ending, with our narrator and his doubts about Michael: "I've heard him say this before, but now . . . I wonder if even he believes it" (229). An open question.

And another, with Mary and Michael, embracing. The sentence begins with a turn: "But his eyes, rather than catch the camera, focus somewhere in the distance over Mary's head, their irises highlighted by sloping sunshine. They merge with the exploded dots of gray and blue" (231). As if there were more to be told. As if he were an image in a photograph, or a figure in a novel.

*

With its non-linear structure, multiple points of view and the art image in the title, *Figures on a Wharf* sets aside many of the conventions of landscape fiction, even while it builds on the strengths of the realist tradition: a solidity of specification, an awareness of the importance of fine detail and the power of accumulation. Yet Tefs creates a world in which the players make their own fates, rather than wait for them to be delivered from the clouds. He challenges the reader to participate in the making of things, to hear the double voice of the narrative, to join the company, and break bread together. He leaves room for the reader's imagination and intelligence to play, opens things up, admits play, and playing is a good thing, to admit such play is a good thing, and so is this novel.

Works Cited

Burnett, David. *Colville*. Toronto: McClelland and Stewart, 1983.

Dow, Helen J. *The Art of Alex Colville*. Toronto: McGraw-Hill Ryerson, 1972.

Fiedler, Leslie. *Love and Death in the American Novel*. Revised Edition. New York: Delta, 1966.

Findley, Timothy. *The Wars*. 1977. Harmondsworth: Penguin, 1978.

Forster, E.M. *Aspects of the Novel*. 1927. Harmondsworth: Penguin, 1962.

Harrison, Charles Yale. *Generals Die in Bed*. 1930. Hamilton: Potlach, 1974.

Kroetsch, Robert. *What the Crow Said*. Toronto: General, 1978.

Tefs, Wayne. "The Aussies: From Outback to Paperback." *Border Crossings* (Spring 1989): 56-57.

__________. *The Canasta Players*. Winnipeg: Turnstone Press, 1990.

__________. *The Cartier Street Contract*. Winnipeg: Turnstone Press, 1985.

__________. "Current Prairie Fiction: Openings/Beginnings." *Border Crossings* (Winter 1985): 55-56. Rpt. in *Trace: Prairie Writers on Writing*. Ed. Birk Sproxton. Winnipeg: Turnstone Press, 1986. 241-48.

__________. *Figures on a Wharf*. Winnipeg: Turnstone Press, 1983.

__________. "The Hayseed Factor in Prairie Fiction." *Border Crossings* (Winter 1990): 45-46.

__________. "Travels with Mrs. Torture." *Border Crossings* (Summer 1989): 22-23.

Decentering the Text: Transgression and Dialogue in Dennis Cooley's *Bloody Jack*

Debbie D'Aoust

> Once we begin to lose faith in an aesthetic that recognizes, even celebrates, systems of ascribed superiority, we begin to remake our poetics. We may no longer esteem the poet as a master who imposes order or, god-like, manipulates language. We are not so readily convinced then that poetry must be written in a foreign idiom, as though it were written solely by and (often, it seems) for dead Englishmen. We no longer feel compelled to write or read 'universal' texts and 'eternal' truths. We no longer believe there are verities outside a place and moment of conception. Or reception. (Try *Hamlet* on Australian aborigines.) (Cooley, *Vernacular Muse* 179)

The postmodern decentering impulse is often associated with an aesthetic of absence, which seeks to efface all boundaries, to reject all attempts to formulate difference, and thus to deny the possibility of there even existing a "place and moment"—a local(e)—out of which one could write. Another variety of the decentering impulse, which has been important for many prairie writers, aims not at just any sort of positive content, but at privileged instances of presence, opposed to those we might locate as marginal or peripheral. This version, less extreme in one sense, but more politically powerful in another, builds on the recognition that supposed "universals" are really just ideological constructs, and that, fundamentally, there are only locals, whose values are not inherent, but relative and culturally determined. Seen from this theoretical angle, writing out of one's own "place and moment" may represent a rebellion against the authority which has attempted to impose its own values by making one local central.

An interesting mixture of both types of decentering impulses may be seen at work (and play) in Dennis Cooley's *Bloody Jack*. In neither version is one centre merely replaced with another. Rather, Cooley's text challenges and deconstructs the very notion of "a centre," with this term being variously construed as either presence or ideological construct. This creative energy manifests itself primarily through the activities of transgression and dialogue. The transgression of conventional textual boundaries releases voices and opens spaces in the discursive field in which they may engage in dialogue. In turn, by questioning traditional notions of unity and identity (of genre, work, theme, history, truth, character, author, and so on), these activities function to fundamentally decenter the text.

One possible, and perhaps appropriate, way to begin an exploration of this process is with the text's cover, which categorizes the text generically as "a book." A quick flip through its pages reveals the necessity of such a general term, for it contains a wide sampling of genres of both poetry and prose (both what we would recognize as fiction and nonfiction), as well as a musical score, a budget report, and a number of items that defy easy categorization. Examples of these "hybrid" items are "the yard" (4-6) and "cunning linguist" (77-87) which slip back and forth between poetry and prose, "Criminal Life" (98) which could be read as a poem or as a title page in the nineteenth-century novel style, and "IOU (Laws Line of Credit)" (185) which appears to be a picture made out of letters.

Another item, a letter to Krafchenko from his "jipsylady," transgresses the notion that book-matter must be typeset, by being handwritten in what Krafchenko calls "childish lettering" (64). It also crosses and blurs the line between "illiterate" and "poetic" writing: "once I dremt how you wuld tutsch me close and we wuld roll on the bed was warm and all over your hands and your eyes your eyes my love" (221). We have, then, not only a transgression of traditional boundaries between genres and styles, but also *within* them. If identity is a construct of difference, and a product of exclusion, then what we have here is an explosion of the very notion of the identity of a genre or style. Discourse is redefined and revalued in terms of what it includes rather than what it excludes, and the book opens into a dialogue of discourses which traditionally are segregated. *Bloody Jack*'s author is like the *corvus brachyrhynchos*: "an opportunist in its feeding / it will eat almost anything" (73).

In case we miss this new principle on our own, we are alerted to it by the book's inclusion of an epigraph by Julia Kristeva from her essay "Word, Dialogue, and Novel" in which she summarizes Mikhail Bakhtin's discussion in *Problems of Dostoevsky's Poetics* of Menippean discourse and its all-inclusive nature. The Menippea (and Cooley's "book") may be seen as a new (historically very old) genre constituted by the mixing of other genres and styles. It does have an "identity," but one that eschews a centre, and is defined only in terms of inclusion rather than exclusion. The Menippea can thus never be totally satisfied or "completed," as there will always be something more that could be added to it. It will resist its textual boundaries, and call attention to their arbitrary nature. Hence *Bloody Jack* appears to "end" only because it is bar-room closing time: "*O.K., that's about it. Closing time folks.*

Drink up. / empties rattling. *Can you drink up there. Closing,* / *sorry*" (236).

The presence of this Kristeva epigraph functions in a number of other ways as well, one of which is to give us our first hint that in this book we, as readers, will not be alone. One or another version of Cooley is with us throughout, calling into question conventional notions of the autonomy of authors, readers and texts, and inviting a high degree of interactivity. For instance, in "appendix," the last item in *Bloody Jack*, we are first given a brief lesson in anatomy and then addressed directly: "Perhaps, dear reader, you would like to remove this appendix. Go ahead, just cut it out. You always wanted to be a doctor, here's your chance" (237). If the use of epigraphs has commonly been an acceptable way for an author, using another's words, to try to guide a reader's reading, the direct address has not (at least not since preferences that authors "show" rather than "tell" hardened into dogma).

Indeed, critic Smaro Kamboureli identifies such manoeuvres as Cooley's "transgression of his writing role." Taking the voice of "you have my word" to be the poet's, she states that he is "stealing my privilege as reader, by inscribing my reading in his text" (17). In traditional terms, not only should writers stay out of the text, but they should leave reading out of it, too. By crossing these boundaries Cooley opens a space for dialogue between at least three parties: author, reader and text. I say at least three, because the voice in "you have my word" could also be read as that of the titular outlaw Jack Krafchenko, as his refusal to be captured in words by the journalistic authorities who would try to make him "one of their characters" (16). In his insistence that "you cant see me on the page" (17) he rejects the fiction of all "realist" writing (including that which calls itself non-fiction), and positions himself outside words: "to find me / you must read be / tween the lines" (18).

Krafchenko's rejection of the authority of others' discourse (here this must also include Cooley's) to de-scribe him parallels the sentiment expressed in two other epigraphs included in the book: "To rob a man of his language in the very name of language: this is the first step in all legal murders" by Roland Barthes, and "Not a story about me through their eyes then" from Michael Ondaatje's *The Collected Works of Billy the Kid*, and spoken in the first person by Billy. Notice that I said these epigraphs are included within the *book*. Oddly, they appear to lie in a nether land between the cover and the beginning of the "text," as signalled by page numbering. Counting backwards from page three, where the first poem "dear valentine" is found, we find that page one, the beginning of the text, is the dedication "to Penny" (one of Krafchenko's lovers). The epigraphs precede this, and are in turn preceded by a page containing "with thanks to," "acknowledgements," and "sources," preceded by copyright information, two title pages, and the cover.

This curious fact might either escape our notice or be dismissed as trivial, except that the last of the four epigraphs, "cld fool the bastards," is the first line of the poem "light headed," in which Krafchenko imagines defying gravity and "rising for once & / all in the world" (165). Just as Krafchenko has insisted that he "exists" outside the text, so here his words exist outside the text. His "text" too has defied gravity, risen up and migrated to its margins. To complicate matters, while the first three epigraphs are attributed to the authors of books (Kristeva, Barthes and Ondaatje), this one is attributed to *Bloody Jack*. As all the names are given in italics, there is confusion in the last between book and character, or between character and author; perhaps all three collapse into one.

To complicate matters even further, I said earlier that the Kristeva epigraph is from an essay in which she summarizes Bakhtin; what she actually does is appropriate, without footnoting, a broad collection of his ideas and phrasings. The parallels between Kristeva's and Bakhtin's language are at times so close as to suggest that their only differences may have been introduced by their respective translators.

Cooley, writing elsewhere, links our sense of such borrowings as inappropriate with an economic system and print culture which views books as commodities:

> the word "plagiarism" did not enter the language until after the Renaissance and has no etymology, at least no recorded history before that. A neologism—like "ecology" in the Romantic period—manufactured to fit a new sense of 'fact' and value, it has taken us for the last few centuries away from the sense of a shared language whose ingredients were openly available in a kind of verbal communism. (*Vernacular Muse* 200)

Cooley is not here advocating plagiarism (his own essays are extensively footnoted), but drawing our attention to the fact that plagiarism is a culturally endorsed construct, which seeks, in a rather artificial way, to ascribe ownership to words and ideas.

Since we have noted that Bakhtin (through Kristeva, through Cooley) is already involved in the "text" (broadly construed) under discussion, we may as well take this one step further and introduce Tzvetan Todorov's discussion of Bakhtin's dialogical principle. Todorov notes that although Bakhtin often used the term dialogism to designate a privileged instance of itself, he also used the term in a much broader sense in which *all* discourse is dialogic. This more general sense depends on the observation that all utterances are related to all other utterances because all words (except, I might note, certain neologisms on their early appearance) have "always already been used" and thus "carry within themselves the traces of preceding usage" (60-64). In other words, *all* text is intertextual, and the notion that any text, no matter how extensively footnoted, documents its sources fully is a fiction.

All this has the effect of further calling into question our notions of "the text" and "the author" and the "boundaries" or "identities" of each. If epigraphs are traditionally the place where authors say something using another's words, in *Bloody Jack* these distinctions begin to break down in a web of intertextuality: we find Ondaatje using (ostensibly) Billy the Kid's language, Krafchenko using (essentially) Cooley's language, Kristeva using ("plagiaristically") Bakhtin's language, the book using (reflexively) the text's language, and Barthes using (as far as I know) his own language to speak of the terror of being "accused, deprived of language, or worse, rigged out in that of our accusers, humiliated and condemned by it." The point is, I think, not to try to untangle this web, but to realize that before the text of *Bloody Jack* has even (supposedly) begun, Cooley has presented a situation in which the reader may activate and participate in a multi-dimensional dialogue with at least ten distinct participants.

Countless other participants enter when we begin reading forward into the numbered pages, but before we do so it should be noted that the present number (ten) more than quadruples if we extend our reading back one page to include the voices of the significant others named there. Who knows what influence those other writers, colleagues, friends, family members, implied publishers, editors, and so on in the sections "with thanks to" and "acknowledgements" may have had on the words and ideas that appear in this book? The notion of a singular, isolated and isolable, self-contained author is here being challenged, as it is in the section "sources" which begins "I have taken and often modified material from several sources" and then lists a newspaper and a number of books.

Of course, once the boundaries of the text have been called into question who knows whether the "debts" to people and texts listed on this page are real or fictional? Or if the people and texts themselves are real or fictional? By transgressing and confusing the boundaries between the original and the modified, or the authentic and the forged, Cooley not only allows a dialogue between them to emerge, but also problematizes the distinction between them. For instance, the poem "you have my word" challenges us to see that the version of character or story presented in the supposed "sources" is no more real or true than the version Cooley presents. Krafchenko tells us

> they think
> they have me
> where they want me
> that theyve got me
> typed the body shouts & glides
> is shortened in their head
> lines laid out
> even as headstones in the prose
> the deadlines of the daily press (16)

Even if Cooley is "trying to set things / right" (112), in neither version is Krafchenko captured in or by words. Nor can he be, because of the split between signifiers and signifieds, or, to quote a more poetic rendering of this linguistic fact from Cooley's *Perishable Light*,

> because a word spreads & slides
> like cheez whiz
> never lines up
> with the world . . . (55)

The lines are, in this sense, truly "dead"—they contain nothing living or of life—and reference can no longer be taken as the centre of the text.

Once freed from the tyranny of meaning, the text is free to engage in dialogue with itself. Words are free to engage in self-reflexive play, hence the emergence of the pun as a predominant stylistic trope. This play also manifests itself as a delight in sounds for their own sake, as in the poem "Kessa" with its mesmerizing repetitions and slippery syntax: "come on over here come to me come to see me come here come / on pussycat oh she is so dainty yes she is so pretty so yes / such a nice pussy arent you Kessa come on come here come on" (*Bloody Jack* 88). Of course, not all readers will be amused by either type of play. Cooley, again in *Perishable Light*: "you want significance / you are wondering / how did this poem get published" (13). Within *Bloody Jack* the aesthetics of language play are associated with an oral tradition in which the fact that a speaker "dint say a hell a lot come to think of it, a lot of the time" (10) does not diminish the value of the speech itself.

To return to the issue of Cooley's "sources," we see that by transgressing the boundary between history and fiction Cooley calls into question the distinction between them, and challenges the idea of "truth" as a discursive centre. As Linda Hutcheon has said, "History (like fiction) is constructed, systematized, and given meaning by its writers and its readers. The past is not coherent, continuous, and unified—until we make it so" (36). *Bloody Jack* asks, I believe, that we not make it so. This is evident because we are not provided with a single coherent version of Krafchenko and his crimes, narrated from a single coherent point of view, but rather a plurality of versions, each representing a different point of view. For example, we hear from the police, a CBC journalist, an anonymous writer, some of the men of the community, the printed press, Krafchenko himself, an acquaintance Karen Long, an indignant Nellie L. McClung, and Dr. Normal L. Braun, criminal psychologist, to name only a few.

The presence of such a plurality of competing voices and viewpoints, and the absence of a single overriding one which negates or confirms the others, is consistent with a view of history as incoherent and fragmented. It is also a feature of what Bakhtin called a "polyphonic" work. Bakhtin describes the writer of polyphony as one who

> creates not voiceless slaves (as does Zeus), but *free* people, capable of standing *alongside* their creator, capable of not agreeing with him and even of rebelling against him. . . . *not only objects of authorial discourse but also subjects of their own directly signifying discourse.* (6-7)

What is at issue here is, as Wayne Booth puts it in his introduction to Bakhtin's work, whether the author allows "voices into the work that are not fundamentally under the 'monological' control of the novelist's own ideology" (xx).

The Barthesian epigraph on the horror of being "deprived of language, or worse, rigged out in that of our accusers," and the epigraph "spoken" by Billy the Kid, "Not a story about me through their eyes then," suggest that such monological control is not only antithetical to the inclusive principle of *Bloody Jack*, but also an authorial (authoritarian) crime. Authorial control can never be completely relinquished in a text, but the strategies of polyphony, itself a type of authorial design, may be seen as a movement in that direction. Rather than attempt to "erase" himself as author, as *subject* of his discourse, Cooley adopts a split identity and inscribes himself as *object* in the discourse of his text. This "other self," a quantity perhaps similar to what we often speak of as an author's "persona," is then further split into speaking subject, which can enter into dialogue with the book's other voices, and silent object, which can function as the "topic" of the other voices' discourse.

"Cooley" as silent object appears in the piece "what the crow really said," in which an outspoken crow advises Krafchenko, much as a publishing agent would, on the directions in which he should take the book. Meanwhile, the crow informs us, "Cooley" has been relegated to the role of recorder:

> Has it not occurred to you that Mr. Cooley, who this very moment, as you and I converse, nay—discourse—at this very moment, that he himself is hurting? That even as these exchanges take place he must stab at this typewriter in his inimicably stupid way? (179)

It soon emerges that Krafchenko fears "Cooley" may be transgressing his transcriber's role, his role as "object," and taking on a role as "subject" (or "actor") within the discourse. Krafchenko confides to the crow: "cooley hes bin buggin me see you know tryin to interfere take / credit away from me like i think hes fallen in love with penny & / hes trying to get her into the sack . . ." (180). Once the boundaries of "the text" have been dissolved, just about anything is possible.

Given this open antagonism between our "author" and his "hero," it is no wonder that in "high drama," when "Cooley" (as subject) tries to direct a love scene between Krafchenko and Penny, Krafchenko tells him to "Butt out buddy. It's none of your business" (222). In this scene it appears that "Cooley" does eventually get his way, but only after the members of his "cast" have engaged in a small revolt against their "objectification" by him (asserting their own subjectivity within the discourse), and at the expense of making himself as subject (and the idea of monological control) appear childish and tyrannical.

Another way in which the principle of polyphony serves to "decenter" the author is through the inclusion of various local voices which are presented as counters to Cooley's potentially hegemonic position. Two items in the book are, perhaps, the most obvious instances of this. The first is a letter addressed "Dear Editor" from (MRS.) Agnes Klassen, the second is a book review, ostensibly from the *Times Literary Supplement*, titled "Subversive Only in a Hyphenated Sense" by L.A. Wynne-Smith. Both are dated in 1984, the year of *Bloody Jack*'s publication, and although neither names this book in its remarks we are invited, I believe, to read both as reactions to it (giving us, interestingly, an already read text). Both are openly negative, even hostile.

Klassen accuses Cooley of "cynical aetheist attacks on what has made Canada what it is today," says she "wouldn't be surprised if he votes NDP," and professes to be shocked and disgusted by his language: "The words are bad enough but every time I reread those passages I find more and more obscenity shoved down my throat. Sex everywhere. Its crawling with sex" (89). Klassen's comments may be thick with ironies (depending on the *reader's* viewpoint), but this does not undermine the fact that they may be read as representing plausible and authentic "upright" responses to a transgressive text such as this one. The author of the book review (whose initials, L.A.W.S., are telling) is credited with a number of similarly "authentic" statements:

> Such raids on the intelligent, and intelligible, shapes of language should no longer be taken seriously. In these verses there is no genuine effort to reach the best in us. . . . Lamentably, one finds no character in this book, no real character that is—one which is fully and causally realized. . . . What is wanting is something more human, certainly more humane. Above all, we need writers who speak in full intelligence to the fears and desires of the race. (142)

Again, depending on the reader's viewpoint, these statements based on ready-made post-Romantic "laws" of poetry may or may not appear ironic.

It might be argued, of course, that much more subtle, interesting and devastating critiques of *Bloody Jack* than Klassen's and Wynne-Smith's are possible, and that by including only examples of such lazy, conservative criticism in his book Cooley is actually *enhancing* his authorial control, by defining (and hence limiting) hostile reactions to his book. The fact is, however, that such lazy, conservative dismissals of poets and poetry perceived to be "radical" in some way have long been staples of certain prominent schools of Can.Lit. criticism. What is interesting about these hostile voices is that Cooley, by transgressing the boundaries of the text, is able to open a space in the discursive field in which they may join in the ongoing dialogue as, to repeat Bakhtin's phrase, "*not only objects of authorial discourse but also subjects of their own directly signifying discourse*." The dialogic status of all the voices in *Bloody Jack* (including "Cooley's"), the fact that all are both object and subject, opens the way for an incredible amount of ambivalent play.

Of course, it must be recalled that polyphony does not

involve the absence of authorial design, and that earlier I spoke of discourse being revalued in terms of what it includes rather than what it excludes. If we locate *Bloody Jack*'s design in a decentering impulse which operates in conjunction with a poetics of inclusion, then the voices which are devalued within the book (those which we will be most likely to read as objects of parody) will be those which (as subjects) attempt to impose a rigid centre that would exclude and silence other voices. For instance, the voices of both Klassen and Wynne-Smith appear inappropriate or distasteful precisely because they seek to silence most (if not all) the other voices in the book. This revaluation extends even to cover "author" and "hero"—"Cooley" appears childish and tyrannical when he attempts to control the voices of Krafchenko and Penny (222), and Krafchenko appears at his worst when he proves unwilling to talk over his disputes with the crow "in a civilized manner" (180).

Similarly, the "Law" is devalued when it is revealed to be a local value system, masquerading as a universal centre, which silences opposing voices by imposing its language upon them. As the judge trying Krafchenko's case tells the jurors:

> The common jury has long been regarded as the palladium of British liberty, and it will hold that high place in public confidence just so long as it can be depended upon, *in the language of your oath*, a true verdict to give according to the evidence. . . . For the law as it stands neither you nor I have any responsibility. (49, emphasis mine)

Despite the dissenting voices of some of the men of the community and that of Nellie McClung, it appears that Krafchenko is something of a local hero—so much so that the judge must warn the jury about "weak sentimentality" interfering with a "true verdict" (49). Krafchenko's localness is also presented as a particularly marginal sort, for as immigrant, as one of the "class of foreigners that was thrust upon" the province (116), he is viewed as an "import." It is ironic, then, that his chief antagonist, the British-derived justice system, is also an import. This discrepancy, in fact, represents a classic case of one "local" being promoted by the powers that be to the status of "universal," with claims of inherent value, and another "local" being assigned a position on the periphery, and its being denied even relative value.

It should be apparent by this point that both Cooley and Krafchenko are outlaws—"outside" of laws that are revealed, through their transgression, to be social, political and ideological constructs, declared to be central by the authority of Others. As Cooley has said, "This [the Prairie Provinces] is a world where many of us identify with those on the outside or edge because historically that's where we have been put" (Lenoski 169). Cooley's co-founding of Turnstone Press opened spaces into which many prairie voices (including his own) could be released. *Bloody Jack*, I have suggested, may be seen as a discursive parallel to this "real world" activity. By breaking the literary law of the centre, by transgressing traditional narrative, poetic, historical and textual boundaries, the book simultaneously releases a multiplicity of voices and provides a discursive space in which they may enter into dialogue. The "book" enters the carnivalesque realm of the Menippea, which, in Bakhtin's words, destroys "the epic and tragic wholeness of the world" (117), replaces it with "the *joyful relativity* of all structure and order, of all authority and all (hierarchical) position" (124), and, above all, permits "*free and familiar contact among people* . . . a *new mode of interrelationship between individuals*" (123).

Works Cited

Bakhtin, Mikhail. *Problems of Dostoevsky's Poetics*. Trans. Caryl Emerson. Minneapolis: University of Minnesota Press, 1984.

Cooley, Dennis. *Bloody Jack*. Winnipeg: Turnstone Press, 1984.

__________. *Perishable Light*. Regina: Coteau Books, 1988.

__________. *The Vernacular Muse: The Eye and Ear in Contemporary Literature*. Winnipeg: Turnstone Press, 1987.

Hutcheon, Linda. "Challenging the Conventions of Realism: Postmodernism in Canadian Literature." *Canadian Forum* 66.758 (April 1986): 34-38.

Kamboureli, Smaro. "Stealing the Text: George Bowering's *Kerrisdale Elegies* and Dennis Cooley's *Bloody Jack*." *Canadian Literature* 115 (Winter 1987): 9-23.

Kristeva, Julia. "Word, Dialogue, and Novel." *Desire in Language: A Semiotic Approach to Literature and Art*. Trans. Thomas Gora, Alice Jardine, and Leon S. Roudiez. New York: Columbia University Press, 1980. 64-91.

Lenoski, Daniel S. "Voicing Prairie Space: Interview with Dennis Cooley." *Line* 7/8 (Spring/Fall 1986): 166-83.

Todorov, Tzvetan. *Mikhail Bakhtin: The Dialogical Principle*. Trans. Wlad Godzich. Minneapolis: University of Minnesota Press, 1984.

Notes on Birk Sproxton's *Headframe:*

Dennis Cooley

*

An irreverent book, this one. Look at all those slangy expressions. Two men in a part called "Phantom Lake," stricken with love, seem in perfect position for high romance and the special language it might command. "Poetry" even. Here is what we get: "They fought over her / and one bashed the other / over the head" (58). "Bashed"? He "*bashed*" his rival? That's *it*? Hardly the stuff of high romance. Scarcely the lyrical power—nuanced rhythm, original metaphor—we might look for in love poetry. We may be dismayed too at Sproxton's treatment elsewhere of Chatique, "the Pelican," who with his tribe intercepts Alexander Henry in his expedition through what was to become northern Manitoba: "the villagers were ready for a party, a hell of a smash, met Henry's bunch on the shore" (48). The situation Sproxton describes involves a very risky confrontation which could easily lead to something more, but he chooses to speak of it in smart-ass words. It's "Henry's bunch" (not "Alexander's men," a phrase which would be more formal and honorific), and it's "a hell of a smash." Sounds like a folksy story-teller, doesn't he?

Do you want to know about two of the chief characters in *Headframe:*, the two who found the original ore body the mining town of Flin Flon was founded on? Want to know what they do, the figures we might expect to arrive in a book of sources and history with some dignity, some mark of high endeavour? No such chance: "When they stopped on the lake to piss, Tom had the advantage." The text hardly allows them large seriousness when it speaks of the men taking a piss. The two of them mark their presence in the North like dogs, literate dogs, inscribe themselves, however fleetingly, into the northern snow. Tom

> could finish, underline it, and sometimes, on a warmer night, draw a circle, Tom in the centre. But David had trouble. Do you dot the i as you go, or pray for enough pressure to dot it after that last damned painful curving d? (75)

That's not all, not nearly enough. The narrator extends the joke in comic bravado, comments on the exercise: "Never underestimate the pleasures of a short name" (75). At every turn Sproxton jokes, laughs, speaks of his subjects with ribald mockery, unseemly lightness.

*

Then there are all the prosaic entries. What are they doing here? What do they have to do with poetry? And is this a poem, really? On we go, and we run smack-dab into page after page of straightforward language, unelevated words, syntax that refuses in its rhythms to be pretty or 'poetic.' We learn about what the narrator did as a kid growing up in Flin Flon, hear what work the men did in the mines and in bush camp, read several reports on drilling exploration, discover what other people have written about Flin Flon—all this in the most unassuming prose.

*

A strange book this *Headframe:*. What are we to make of all these entries, so varied in form and purpose? There are songs, documents, reminiscences, lists, jokes, tall tales, numbers and names, speculations, definitions, comments on the text (sometimes in the form of marginal glosses, more often in parenthetical asides). There are newspaper reports, pieces of literary criticism, anecdotes, journal entries, primitive film scripts, title pages from other books, snatches from popular songs (most of them from the mid-1950s to the late 1950s). There are extracts lifted from other literature, too, echoes of many other writers. We get Robert Kroetsch, mainly, Kroetsch is all over the place. Maybe too much Kroetsch, crouched there, page after page, in ambush. That's not all, there are others: Robert Frost, David Arnason, Andy Suknaski, William Carlos Williams, Ernest Hemingway, F.R. Scott, Douglas Durkin, Alden Nowlan, W.O. Mitchell, Glen Sorestad, Northrop Frye. He pulls them in, Sproxton takes them over. All these writers and a clutch of other ones, less literary writers, listed at the back of the book. They become part of Sproxton's *Headframe:*, itself one of many texts, only the latest text, to traverse the ground. Flin, who has escaped from his original novel to give birth to other texts, to be a character in them, Sproxton's included,

> stepped
> into a community of songs and novels
> and love stories
> on everyone's
> lips (90)

So the writer snuggles up to others as source, as warmth, puts no stock in himself as isolated and sole creator.

The wild range of words, the grab-bag of mixed discourse, make this a book we read with some effort. Not that the entries themselves are hard to read (they seldom are). The trouble comes in knowing how we are to receive them: can he do this, write this prosy stuff, in poetry I mean? and how good is it, really? The trouble comes in knowing how to relate all the parts: how do the bits and pieces hold together, what do they have in common? Sproxton writing, facetiously, quotes a Canada Department of Mines Summary Report on rock formations in his territory. There are "narrow bands," fragments which are "exceptionally well-exposed," "agglomerates," "interlayered" rocks (35). What is "mined" turns out to be "minding," we then discover in the next section. A clue: the two brought together, mined and mining, as comparable actions presumably. Another clue, same page: "letters," "this word," "other letters," a father's baseball uniform "said *Mine* a place I did not own and had never been to and learned about in bits and pieces" (35). Poetics, then, a statement about poetics in this lettered and verbalized world. Metalingual. "Mine," a place, being brought by fragments into possession, becoming "mine," what the poet owns, what is by birthright his.

What *is* this book, then? How do we read it? And how do we evaluate it? These are questions we ask ourselves.

*

So, where do we start? Anywhere would be fine, we could open it anywhere. Since this is a book that gives no simple narrative line or progression, anywhere would do. But to begin at the beginning. Right from the start we see the book struggling to come into existence. First words, slangy words: "*What are you doing in there?* shouts my father banging on the bathroom door. *Homesteading?*" (3). Yeah, the home place, where you get your start. Where you live. If you live there (in the north) long enough, "you know what is where, and where is here" (124). Sneaky reply to Northrop Frye who has argued that the essential Canadian question is: "Where is here?"

That is where the book begins, here with prairie idiom, narrator positioned as bungler, fumbler. Fool. Father as artful speaker, part of a new poetry which is neither learned nor fastidious. There is more. This is "a place to be in, / a place / to begin" (3). To begin, then, is to be in. The rhyme brings the expressions into line. A beginning then, one rooted in a place, a being there. Fine, books can start with a beginning, they often do. First things first. All right, let's go with that.

But wait a minute, these are no known beginnings, certainly no common beginnings, these stutterings toward language. We may well have father endowing the son (provoking him?) with speech, bringing him into it in comical parody perhaps of god the father and his son.

mmmmmmmmm

aaaaaaaaa

mmmmmmmmmmm

aaaaaaaaaaa (3)

We recognize the sounds, comically, scatologically, as signs of difficulties for the speaker, working in so fundamental a position. Grunts, wheezes—these are the most basic sounds, something short, I suppose, of articulate speech. But straining toward it.

First sounds then. Ursounds. Babble. Baby talk. You see where this takes you. Poet finds a beginning, utters his first sounds, nonsense maybe, but it's a beginning, it's a start. Baby steps. Not bad for starters. A breathing toward speech. As we discover later in the book, this whole world for which Flin Flon is synecdoche lies at the edges of possibility: "The town lay quiet, gestating, not yet fully imagined into existence" (90). "The town dangles there on the edge of the Laurentian shield at the end of the line, an infant, and at the mother end: a novel/navel" (113). Begotten by words, in the novel navel from which it emerges. Gestating, gesticulating, gesturing toward speech, that's our narrator. He is working his way toward story, as we soon discover. Something Adamic, then, about these stutterings, first attempts to speak and name (and this book is rife with namings and awareness of naming). Even as the thought might scandalize some readers, might offend them, the Biblical structure is surely there: the son, beckoned by the father, attempts to speak. He attempts, too, as subsequent pages make clear, to name the creation, even though he knows names will not hold, no names will suffice. A prairie Genesis then, one of many texts these days to explore a first speaking in the prairies, a speaking of it in the face of 'foreign' words and models.

How do you grow a prairie poet? Robert Kroetsch asks in *Seed Catalogue*. How do you grow a Flin Flon poet? Sproxton asks.

As later he seeks another "opening," a place to be in, to begin. You open a mine, you open a book (114, 94). Same thing.

*

Supposing we read the passage, that cluster of m's and a's, in a more linguistic way, one that perhaps would not depend so fully upon knowledge of other literary texts. What then? One consonant, one vowel. The makings of anything there? One vowel, one consonant, and we have got meaning or the possibility of meaning in English. Phoneme. So we connect them. ma? am? mama? am am? Something there surely. A being (I "am"?), a mothering or a calling on mother ("ma" and "mama"), being brought to life, nurtured in our mother's tongue. We may well feel empowered to try on these possibilities, given the rudimentary scatter of letters before us, given the overt gloss the narrator provides for us (to be in, to begin)—one which we may receive both as direction and as invitation. We feel justified, too, by invoking a convention I have already mentioned, namely the Adamic one which endows our literary books with such awareness.

There are other conventions we might call upon: that of starting a book or a text—especially an ambitious poem, such as this one, one that would take on tribal significance—with some kind of invocation, some calling upon basic powers. A kind of prayer, a prairie prayer possibly. If we read this opening in retrospect, that is with the rest of the book in mind, we may feel confirmed in these suppositions, for we later discern how crucial the mother is to the book as source of life.

One further thought. The speaker is in the position I have been describing, maybe. He is musing, searching for words. Isn't that what we say as we stall for time, wait for a word to come to us? It's "mmmm," let me think about that: "mmmm." And it's, well, you know, it's "aaaa," gimme a minute it will come to me, don't rush me, "aaa." We say these things, expressively, when we wait for articulate speech to reach us. We want to show we are trying. It's like sitting in Germany & you hardly know a word of German and you try to squeeze something out. You can imagine what that's like.

*

Beginnings. Thoughts of home. "Night Thoughts on the Home Place" Sproxton has titled this first page (3). Parody of Robert Browning? of Robert Kroetsch, he who in *Seed Catalogue* wrote of beginnings, of finding a voice, growing a poet in the prairies, on the home place?

You want starters? Turn the page and there's another—earth in cataclysmic eruption, the beginnings of something big. Another straining, "straining the earth" (4), this event marks yet another start. The first was local and idiomatic, this is geological and (mainly) technical: "basic" and "acidic" and "granitic" (in visual likeness to the "gantic" "magma"). It is comical too: this is one big mama who gives birth to magmas. (Do we hear, are we asked to hear "mama" talking inside that word "magma"?)

A breathing on the first page, a birthing here. In the

contamination of the text, in its evident and increasing propensity to mix elements, we begin to make the connections.

The second birth passage again echoes Genesis, except here the reverberations are unmistakable. Once the earth gives birth, "she sees it is good / and takes her rest" (4). Just before this we see how "on the seventh / granitic magmas rise" (4).

*

The following pages pick up the note and extend it. "Tumescence," we learn, is a geological term, whose definition in the text gives rise to sexual innuendo (5). The miners emerge from the dark ground like little kids "clutching / (yes) hugging their lunch pails" (6). The slowness of their emergence, caught in repetitive language, emphasizes a birthing. The text finds new ways to express their emergence, bit by bit:

> dark
> out of the dark
> out of the dark ground (6)

As each line exceeds the previous one and extends still further into the page we begin to recognize the elongations, branching to either side of the base word, as visually expressive of something coming into or rising within our visual field. The lineation works aurally too. The first line falls with a thud: "dark." The modification which follows—"out of the"—tips that beat firmly onto "out." It is "*out* of the dark." And then, in line three, when we add to the right the word "ground," it in turn as new and qualifying word takes over the stress: "out of the dark *ground*." The lineation invites us to read the lines with something like these emphases:

> *dark* [pause for the line end]
> *out* of the dark [second pause]
> out of the dark *ground*

We note that such attention in Sproxton's poetry falls generally on words that open and close lines. The effect is an expressive prosody which in its irregular stressings attends, here, upon a sense of wonder in discovery, each stress registering the speaker's sense of coming upon things and showing those discoveries in the inflection of his voice.

*

So there are entrances. Later on *Headframe:* will pick them up and thicken their possibilities.

It will consolidate in loose accumulation references to mining, to sexuality, and to writing. In this way it builds cohesion and meaning in the poem.

There he is, young protagonist, filling in a mining shaft. Out he goes, armed with (what else?) a long-handled spade. What we read makes him both child coming to mother, and lover (apprehensive lover) impregnating the woman the earth is:

> bellycord stretches & dynamo child pushes
> softsand wary to the earth's dark hole
>   (narrowdeep canal crusted with fine fluxsand)
> & dynamo child shuffles crosstrack
> heaves shovelhandle rightdown leftup
> throws seed for shaftfill
>   fearshiver tingles thru shoulderarmknees (17)

And we remember how the town dangles like a baby. We read, later, how the diamond drill is like a lover. Lyric moment, flow of vowels, all those rhymes at the end:

> waiting for the hunch
> of three-legged lover   warm
> slide of core barrel   engine's
> gentle hum   and the diamond speeding
> seeding water   deep in the sweet dark (59)

Another seeding, male into female, miner into mine. Learn still later how opening a book is like opening a mine, how "the tip of a prospector's pick / (watch how you say that)" opens the book as we (or some of us) open a book, prickish perhaps (94). It is "a refined refinding" (117), these artful acts, when we learn how to read what lies before us—ore or word.

Or word and love and paddling. Everywhere we find linkages: "stroke stroke stroke, *slip*, stroke stroke stroke," where the beating stirs the blood and the words appear, as if in writing, "*slip, stroke, stroke*" (49).

*

Acts of love. These are acts of love. Not perfumy and lavender love perhaps, but love all the same. This love takes its gentlest form in the interludes which occupy several scattered pages toward the beginning of the text and that then reappear toward the end. These moments are among the most lyrical in *Headframe:*, and they circulate small variations upon one another. Generally they use the same few words and they scatter those words more openly on the page than do other sections: deep dark ground sweet in out of earth dream under. Generally they turn in on themselves in rhyme and reverie. They build off a root or base word which they extend or modify, throw us out again and again from that word, yo-yo on a string that keeps bringing us back: "sleep / out of a sleep / out of your earthsleep / out of your deepsleep / out of your sleepsweet" (9). In this way, they develop a strong sense of continuity, even as they allow for small adjustments in which words are used, their combinations, and their setting on the page. The passages serve as expressive song, then, as refrain. They draw attention to the speaker in his lyrical mode. But they work too, don't they, as invocation, a calling into being? Language as charm, a calling upon the muses, the winds of inspiration.

The idea reappears late in the book, bringing the text to some kind of closure, when we learn of the "burden" in a song

(118), together with prairie speech as an "overburden" for a mining poet (121), of the possible "burden" of hauling dirt (123), of the mother renamed Burton who is no "burden" to the poet (131). Refrains everywhere, the book gluing itself together with repetitions and recursions, more and more of them toward the end. However distant the passages may be from one another, we hear in the later ones distinct echoes of what we have read before.

*

What else? What other signs of artfulness? Well there are the men's crude jokes in the bush camps and the mines, for one thing. At times they are corny and 'juvenile,' maybe even crude and obscene, part of Sproxton's willingness to invest in the 'subliterary' and the disreputable. At times they are madly inventive. A whistle at the mine, the Schmidt twins decide, "Honks like a constipated goose" (10). A foreman, noticing a man day-dreaming on the job, asks, "*You gonna stand there like a prick at a wedding?*" (14). A gang burning up old railway ties "burned so many piles Blackie called them the hemorrhoid crew" (8). "Spruce happy"? Spruce happy is when you are "*running thru the bush like a bear cub with his first hard on*" (93). Other times the men's inventiveness takes the form of antics. One time some bush workers "decided to play a little joke by dragging a dead bear into the hotel and propping it up on a toilet in the men's room" (33).

We cannot fail to notice how their imaginations play around the body. Erotic, sure, but anal too. How are we to take that in a serious poem? Anything to do with that opening section, young budding poet, holed up in the can, gasping over his body's refusal to do his bidding, spastically coming into speech? It is there, evidently, in just such moments, unassuming moments, that you start building your poem.

*

You build in an oral way. Prairie way for many poets, especially the male poets. At one point the speaker pauses, in search of something, to say "listen." He can't see the birds he is trying to find, but he can hear them. Plays it by ear. He ends the whole book, lays down a last word that leaves us with the same injunction: "Listen:" (132). (The ending has been "torn out," we learned earlier, is "nowhere to be found" [71].) The ending comes, such as it is, on the last page, after all those pages and pages of words. Here is what we read on the very last page: "To begin with" (132). How clever these words are in their breeziness, in the camouflage they gain in idiom. In the end we begin, we listen, we begin to listen.

Listen? Sure we'll listen. We listen to a narrator who is conspicuous throughout this book. He will often address us in imperatives and pleas. Insists on the second person. "You," yeah you, the text keeps saying. Keeps letting the narrator in, with his modalities and observations, his constant presence. "Stings, don't it?" "Let us therefore . . ." (105). Oral. In oral literature you don't have to disappear, it's you and all those guys you are talking to. Are they taking it to heart? "I guess," he says, this Sproxton narrator, sardonically: "they call Mandy a Glory Hole   I guess / Bramble knew" (50). "Now there's a planting for you" (51), "the crack of dawn as they say" (43), "Anyway, Noah was there" (38)—everywhere the sounds of his presence.

A genial presence. "You know," he says, "You know already that a mining story is a story of love" (76). "I myself have a list of abusive phrases I keep for special situations but you know how it goes" (104). A reassuring host, flattering even, he takes us into his confidence, bypasses the role we often expect of poets—someone thinking out loud, to himself, in no way compromised with the embarrassment of "you."

*

Take all those and's, they're oral too. They're all over the place, no need to quote them. We see how the details, often memories, are rolled into one another within the ampersands. They are separated only minimally by those conjunctions that refuse to discriminate. And so there they are, the items, all those stories, conjugal in the telling, spliced together with equanimity. Oral. This is a style that refuses to subordinate and that wants to rush on with the telling.

*

Repetitions. More orality. The lovely feel of words as they take on heft. They add up. How we going to get the tripod up, a kid asks. "*Sky hooks* Arnold said *Sky hooks*" (27). We can find the breathless rush of ampersands in other passages. Boys running along the CNR tracks, their excitement in the rapid patter of ampersands (129). The litany of a base: out of, out of, out of; some say, some say, some say. Wonderful rhythm of speech.

*

Idioms too. They're oral. Lots and lots of idioms and sayings. The father: you homesteading in there? Something is "a pretty lame answer" (88), the father wants his kids to "Hit the tick" and will himself act "in two shakes of a dead lamb's tail" (121). The language is even slangy. Someone is "a dummy" (85), people "got the heebie-jeebies" (101), "You remember *that stuff* about building your house on rock" (114, emphasis mine). Subliterary, gloriously subliterary.

*

Lists. Lists are part of an oral economy. Short lists, with their bravado: "Flin soon caused a ruckus, a hubbub, a brouhaha" (101). Longer lists. Nicknames:

Christer, Curly-headed
Flycatcher, Ninnie-hammer
Rascal, Mangy
Sleaze-bucket, Fat Mouth

> Twaddletrap, Twittwat
> Whoremonger, Shitsniffing
> Wormsweat, Willywiggle (104)

There's something heroic about that list, a rough inventive energy it contains, a rough street poetry.

*

And you tell stories. Above all you tell stories. That bunch of nicknames, they're stories too, that's what the narrator says: "I think nicknaming is a way of telling a story or making a poem."

> Everyday we tell stories like this—making people into characters for our fictions. Barnyard Ted or Sheepshit Stan or Sidekiss—they're all stories. There may be affection in the stories . . . but mostly we use nicknames to keep people in character. They try to grow and change maybe, but we keep sticking them back into character. (88)

Here in this postmodern text, which scatters language all over the map, refuses the comforts of known or overriding narrative, we hear stories. Sproxton jams them in all over the place, sprays them around like a tomcat. Probably the most dominant in an array of forms is the anecdote. Many of the entries he himself seems to have occasioned involve brief narratives. Even the lists turn into abbreviated narratives. There is one which turns into a sketchy history of the northwest (34), another which kicks in the Orpheus story:

> on their journey he looked back and (so)
> fear
> interest
> concern
> sympathy
> horror
> incredulity (108)

Sometimes the stories are tall tales but they are stories all the same.

Arguably the single most obvious strategy for holding *Headframe:* together is its narrative of a speaker in search of himself (his trip home to Flin Flon—in his mind, and on the road). The loose journey structure—whether in mind or in body—which governs large sections of the poem allows Sproxton to haul in material occasioned by those narratives. He does not limit himself therefore to material which would more obviously fit thematically into the book.

And yet this story does not override everything else. On the contrary, the text disperses to the far corners of the page, tumbles in all directions. Late in the book the text opens a story, a bawdy story about Flin and a lady who babbles about having no tail (there are creatures with no tails in the novel from which the character Flin escaped) and teases us with what might happen. Then there's a halt, one which jabs first at us, then at the narrator himself, self-mocking: "But it didn't happen right away and delay heightens desire so we need an irrelevant chapter which even in a loosely organized work is a challenge and a threat" (107).

*

But you want story, don't you? Well Sproxton's ready for you. He tells a lot of stories, sure, but he keeps talking about stories too. He appropriates a lot of them (from other texts, declares his to be a collective art, postmodern poem). He reports a lot more. Probably invents many but I don't know for sure, and Sproxton's not telling. What is evident, especially in the last section of the book, is an enormous number of explicit references to stories. Metafiction. Throughout *Headframe:* we come across dozens of mentions of the word story, and words such as "read" and "reading" (43 for example), which emphasize this as a composed text with stories to burn: "that's another story" (33), stories about the lake (63), "The story changes a little every time it is told" and "so the story goes" (80). There are so many of these references it would take a whole page just to list them. But you get the idea.

*

So would all the references to names take a long time to enumerate. Little wonder. In a book concerned with starting and knowing and writing, names should have their place. Explorers' names and place names figure most dramatically I suppose. At stake are changed names, attractive names, inappropriate names, identifying names (cultural as well as personal). Could spend some time on that one. Names like "Noah," who "drowns," he actually "drowns" in the winter (40). How about that?

*

Some patterns. Rock. How Sproxton finds and elaborates the word everywhere. You read the rock, at night you dance to rock, you rock, he has rocks in his name Sproxton does, a crow is "raucus."

Steps. People take steps: jogging into The Pas the narrator steps his way, Flin learns to step out of his novel, steps out of a hole in the earth, The Pas was "*le pas*" or "*the stepping place*" (23). The pattern gains special standing when the father counsels his son: "*Take big steps Your shoes will last longer*" (5). It gains perhaps its most telling entry when the narrator tells us that in mining "the hard part is to / find the right step" (16). Right. The right step in other things too, in poetry maybe.

*

We could talk and talk about the book—its use of line for one thing, how telling it is. Take a second on that one. At one point the narrator tells us, sardonically, we "read the story the rock tells / mind the ore take it all" (114). Right, greedy sorts we are, eager readers, we take it *all*. But then, wait, we slip into the next line and read "in." What's this? Oh yeah, we "take it all / in," that too. Works both ways, doesn't it, that "all," a double lining? Fooled too by the lining, we are taken in, the joke is on us, doubly. Another instance. Remember the earth straining to give birth? Well Sproxton breaks up the word "gigantic" so that there is a large gap between "gi" near the left margin and "gantic," to the right and lower. The hole suggests a pausing or stretching across the line which simulates the rhythms of slow eruption (4).

Then there's rhyme, the book's heavy with rhyme. Its allusions (many of them, hidden often behind the hick posing). Its involved sense of form. Clearly this is a sophisticated book, the narrator in the know, however much Sproxton might pose as rustic hick. How dramatic it is, this mix of apparent naïveté and actual sophistication, the interplay of referential language and reflexive structuring. How ridiculously, wonderfully funny it is too, comically inventive, this long prairie poem.

We might read it that way.

Works Cited

Kroetsch, Robert. *Seed Catalogue.* Winnipeg: Turnstone Press, 1977.

Sproxton, Birk. *Headframe:.* Winnipeg: Turnstone Press, 1985.

From "Dying for Love" to "Mrs. Turner": Narrative Control in Stories by Carol Shields

Herb Weil

i

> My first thought this morning is for Beth, how on earth she'll cope now that Ted's left her for the dancer Charlotte Brown. I ask myself, what resources does a woman like Beth have, emotional resources? ("Dying," *Made* 145)

These two sentences begin Carol Shields' "Dying for Love," a story that has been reprinted twice within a year of its original publication (1989). After the first paragraph, the story-teller (perhaps better conceived as what we used to call "the implied author") unobtrusively vanishes—or at least does not explicitly refer to herself until the final paragraphs of the first segment:

> Despite my uneasiness about Beth's ability to cope emotionally, and despite her insomnia, she somehow manages to get up most mornings. . . .
>
> Beth . . . wonders what would happen if she took all

> twelve pills plus the gin. She doesn't know. I don't know either. (148)

This section is the first of three segments in the story. Each is devoted to one woman who may be in danger of dying (because of love or the absence of love). After we learn that Beth empties the gin down the sink and grinds the pills down the garburator, the first segment concludes, "Life is a thing to be cherished, she thinks, and this thought, slender as a handrail, gets her through one more night" (148). Does this last line involve the narrator more intimately than does traditional omniscience? Unnamed, she presents explicitly only feelings, attitudes, and especially worries that are directly relevant to her characters and their situations. (Different readers will quite appropriately weigh differently phrases, rhythms, tones that suggest the technique of leaving insecure any distinctions between teller and creator.) How important is it that Beth and Ted have no last names while Charlotte does? Do all readers sense that the speaker in the second paragraph, partly by revealing intimate details, is *constructing* the characters?

> Habits accrue in that time, especially habits of the night when bodies and their routines get driven into hard rituals of washed skin. . . . Beth curls, but sinuously; her backbone makes a long smiling capital C on the bedsheet, or used to, before Ted told her he was leaving her for Charlotte. (145)

Within this brief story, and in most of her work, Shields creates a wide variety of relations between narrator and characters, situations, actions; between narrator and "implied author"; between each of these and her readers. Often we feel less encouraged to treat the events as if they had happened to the author than we do in other overtly "confessional" fiction, as, for example, by Alice Munro. Nor do we find here the "conspicuously" artificial sub-genre of alleged autobiography—at least in the literal sense best typified by

Machado de Assis in which the speaker (after his own death) tells his story, or more typically, when the narrator is of a gender or an age, or lives in a time, that we know cannot be that of the author. In "Dying for Love" most readers will recognize a very self-conscious narrator, playing with some of the tones implied by her title. How strongly does "dying for" resonate of trite clichés, of transitory pleasures? Do these overtones make it far-fetched to take the phrase literally? Why then does "dying for" rather than "love" dominate in creating the tone?

As we read the story, how convincing are the threats that the cliché-sense will turn into actual death because of what the character, at least, continues to feel is love? But does the narrator feel it as love? Does the author? The second segment begins, "But then there's Lizzie in Somerset; my fears for Lizzie grow day by day. Her predicament is clear and so is her fate, although I would do anything, or almost anything, to assist her in the avoidance of that fate" (148-49). Then the narrator again disappears. Four pages later, in the closing lines of this segment, she returns.

> Who can tell.
>
> One of the advantages in my relationship with Lizzie is my freedom to discard those possibilities she can't yet imagine. All she understands is that both love and the lack of love can be supported. (152)

From the vagueness or false precision of "almost anything" the narrator advances with her character to the finely tuned tone of this final sentence that blends calculation and self-reassurance.

The final, shortest segment begins, "Elsewhere, nearer home, a woman named Elizabeth is lying on her bed in the middle of the afternoon with a plastic dry-cleaner's bag drawn up over her face . . ." (152-53). How important for the reader is the change to the overt absence of the "I" from this sequence until the very last sentence of the story? Surely the first three words of this segment remind any alert reader of her presence. But how firm is the pressure? Need the good reader make much of this? Or of the apparently gratuitous "named"?

The segment and the story end in two long sentences. The first presents the apparently factual—if emotionally loaded—statement, "She is a woman whose life is crowded with not-unpleasant errands . . ." (154). How decisive should we consider the change of tone with the return of the author in the final sentence?

> Not that this is much of a handrail to hang on to—she knows that, and so do I—but it is at least continuous, solid, reliable in its turnings and better than no handrail at all. (154)

Shields encourages many different responses: of hope, of worry, of emphasis upon strengths or upon fragility. In this final sentence, for the first time, the "I" knows precisely what the character knows. The story has moved from an extremely nervous series of questions about another person, allegedly external, with whom the "I" feels strong empathy: "The nights will be terrible for her, I'm sure of that . . ." (145). Does the possible sense that the narrator (as well as the actual author) may have created the characters make her detachment much less? And consequently her handrail much more fragile? We sense here an implied author in a well-controlled but insecure relation to the narrator she has created.

ii

In vivid contrast to Beth, Lizzie, and Elizabeth is the focal character in "Mrs. Turner Cutting the Grass." Few would be less likely to die for love. Unlike the three distinct "heroines" who share variants of the same first name but receive no other, Mrs. Turner seems at first to be captured in that title of address. Not until the third page, after our sense of her has been well established, do we learn that the high school girls on their way home are

> ignorant of that fact . . . that she, Mrs. Turner, possesses a first name—which is Geraldine.
>
> Not that she's ever been called Geraldine. Where she grew up in Boissevain, Manitoba, she was known always—the Lord knows why—as Girlie Fergus. . . . (20)

This story, a frequently anthologized prize-winner and favourite of many of Shields' readers, begins:

> Oh, Mrs. Turner is a sight cutting the grass on a hot afternoon in June! She climbs into an ancient pair of shorts and ties on her halter top and wedges her feet into crepe-soled sandals and covers her red-gray frizz with Gord's old golf cap—Gord is dead now, ten years ago, a seizure on a Saturday night while winding the mantel clock. (18)

At first, this story seems more conventional and familiar than much of the author's recent work. The tone of these first statements seems detached, the unnamed and undescribed narrator hardly sympathetic to her[?] subject. We assume that we are in the world of satire, perhaps of broad comedy (with the temporal jump between sentences), as the story races along with the unencumbered mower:

> The grass flies up around Mrs. Turner's knees. Why doesn't she use a catcher . . . [?] Everyone knows that leaving the clippings like that is bad for the lawn. . . .
>
> . . . [And worse] Roy is far more concerned about the Killex that Mrs. Turner dumps on her dandelions. . . .
>
> . . . But he and Sally so far have said nothing to Mrs. Turner about her abuse of the planet because they're hoping she'll go into an old-folks home soon or maybe die, and then all will proceed as it should.
>
> High-school girls on their way home . . . are mildly, momentarily repelled by the lapped, striated flesh on her upper thighs. . . .
>
> The things Mrs. Turner doesn't know would fill the Saschers' new compost pit, would sink a ship, would set

> off a tidal wave. . . . Back and forth, back and forth she goes with the electric lawn mower, the grass flying out sideways like whiskers. Oh, the things she doesn't know! (18-19)

Smoothly, almost glibly, convincingly, the things Mrs. Turner does not know—not just about grass clippings but about Neil Young, cellulite, "the vocabulary of skin care" (19), the concerns of the chorus of neighbours, and apparently of the narrator—give way to facts that the passing girls and the young parents do not know. Sharply in mid-sentence, the story turns. Until its final paragraph, roughly four-fifths of the story tells us about matters that the girls and the young married couple next door would want to know, but do not even suspect. And finally we learn, too, about the fame of Girlie Fergus, a public persona that she herself does not imagine.

Let us return to look more closely at the major shift in mid-sentence from the "present tense" of an old lady cutting the grass, an old lady so ignorant of facts about contemporary life that she does not even seem to inhabit the same psychological world as any of the unsympathizing characters mentioned. When the narrator moves from the chatty, relaxed, somewhat superior present tense that confidently invites readers to share the story-teller's views, we find the author there waiting to be noticed. There is nothing insistent. Shields gives us a life story that few could have predicted, but which includes only what could well have happened. With the greatest tact, the author creates a past that seems far-fetched but possible. She encourages a range of interpretation: many readers will skim happily along assuming a simple mimetic narrative. Others will feel more aware of an author neatly constructing people and events. The story will work well for both sorts of audience.

In the next paragraph, we quickly learn that Girlie was "the one who got herself in hot water. . . . Girlie got caught one night—she was nineteen—in a Boissevain hotel room with a local farmer, married, named Gus MacGregor" (20). By the next paragraph Girlie has escaped, sneaking out to catch a bus to Winnipeg, another to Minneapolis, to Chicago, to New York City. However wretched the journey, New York is "immense and wonderful" (20). She loves her job as usherette at the Movie Palace in Brooklyn, quickly moves in with "a man named Kiki. . . . His skin was as black as ebony. . . . [She has a baby] boy, rather sweetly formed, with wonderful smooth feet and hands" (21). Deserted by Kiki, she leaves her baby in a beautiful carriage on the porch of a house that "she particularly liked. . . . She has no idea what happened to Kiki . . . [or] to her son" (21-22), but she doesn't worry much. She returns home a year later. Frighteningly embraced and accepted by her family, she quickly leaves to marry "a tongue-tied man . . . who loved every inch of his house. . . . And he loved every inch of his wife, Girlie, too, saying to her once and only once that he knew about her past . . . and that as far as he was concerned the slate had been wiped clean" (22-23). In the single brilliant fast-paced paragraph devoted to this marriage, we learn too of the one time on a passionate picnic when he worshipped Girlie, or at least her body. We barely have time to wonder whether it matters that his sense of knowing all about the past stops at Boissevain. What would he think about New York? What should we?

After Gordon Turner dies, Girlie and her two sisters travel. To Disneyland, to seven countries of Europe, to New Orleans, to Mexico; finally, "three years ago they did what they swore they'd never have the nerve to do: they got on an airplane and went to Japan" (23). This trip and one of its "results," a book of poems, receive the most extensive treatment in the story. Another tourist in the group, the "Professor," a bald, "trim" (24), unsuccessful poet, almost continuously jotting, after his return publishes "a solid little book" (24) which becomes very popular. The favourite poem, always demanded in readings, is his "A Day at the Golden Pavilion":

> [It] was not really about the Golden Pavilion [in Kyoto] at all, but about three midwestern lady tourists who . . . had talked incessantly and in loud, flat-bottomed voices about . . . indigestion, sore feet, breast lumps . . . who back home in Manitoba should receive a postcard. . . . They were the three furies . . . who for vulgarity and tastelessness formed a shattering counterpoint to the Professor's own state of transcendence. . . .
>
> One of the sisters . . . particularly stirred his contempt, she of the pink pantsuit, the red toenails, the grapefruity buttocks. . . . (25)

Always this reading evokes laughter and self-satisfied applause from the students who know "the irreconcilable distance between taste and banality" (26).

Again in mid-paragraph the narrator steps in and corrects her last statement. A new distance combines with a new strong commitment: "Or perhaps that's too harsh; perhaps it's only the difference between those who know about the world and those who don't" (26). Here the distance, strongly reinforced by the assertion that begins the next paragraph—"It's true Mrs. Turner remembers little about her travels. . . . What does it matter? She's having a grand time" (26)—suggests a range of legitimate responses for the readers in deciding the stance and tones of the implied author. The irony toward the youths who already know so much about taste and banality at first offers a range of tones for the implied voice. The revision, "that's too harsh," even modulated by "perhaps," forecloses possibilities, ensuring that with more acute precision we see through the smug students and even more through the self-satisfied poet. (Even Gus MacGregor had received a name—if no physical, social, or other description.)

The three concluding paragraphs return us to the present, primarily in Winnipeg, with an explicit yoking of celebration and irony: "Her sisters have long forgotten about her wild days" (26). To the Local History Museum, Em has donated her father's pipe, her mother's wedding veil, and "a white cotton garment labeled 'Girlie Fergus' Underdrawers . . .' If Mrs. Turner knew the word *irony* she would relish this. Even without knowing the word irony, she relishes it" (27). This past and her "fame" contrast vividly with the way in which the poem brought her, however nameless, into the consciousness of so many audiences. With careful vagueness, the narrator leaves the patronizing professor who has won "an important international award" and who has sold rights to "a number of foreign publishers" (27). Circling to the first six paragraphs, the final one returns to Mrs. Turner. But now, we see things only through her vision—and that created by the narrator—never through that of the high school girls or the neighbours, or, in another world, of the college students. Mrs. Turner waves to the girls (who have become timid), "she hollers hello to Sally and Roy . . . " (27). And finally, the narrator makes overt the vision she shares with her heroine, a vision that Mrs. Turner could never come close to formulating: "She cannot imagine that anyone would wish her harm. All she's done is live her life" (27). Mrs. Turner would never make such claims, but she would no doubt feel pleased, if embarrassed, should she read this description (so unlike the crude ungenerous satiric poem). Only now does the author dare to conclude, with symbolic images and finally with her first explicit celebration: "The green grass flies up in the air, a buoyant cloud swirling about her head. Oh, what a sight is Mrs. Turner cutting her grass and how, like an ornament, she shines" (27).

The author has chosen a subject and created for her a biography that very few of her readers are likely at first to find appealing. She leaves open crucial questions. How can the deserted child, the devoted husband be so quickly dropped? But her movement from satire and irony to the final praise permits her to lead her reader (as Jane Austen did with Emma and Mrs. Bates) away from participating in the narrow-minded alleged superiority of characters early in the story. That we accept as well the contrasting didactic style which the ending incorporates and transforms suggests how skilfully the narrator has earned our trust.

iii

"Mrs. Turner Cutting the Grass" and "Dying for Love" succeed, I think, for most readers, both those who focus upon the strategies of the implied author and those more casual (say, for example, readers sympathetic and alert, but not studying the stories or, at least, not these aspects of the stories). If one attends to the careful timing and tones of authorial control one should have a richer, more complex appreciation, but those only intermittently aware of this craft need never feel excluded from the audience addressed. Two other stories in *Various Miracles*, however, make, in their very distinct ways, much more explicit demands upon their readers. The brief title story (placed first, just before "Mrs. Turner") immediately confronts the reader with the presence of a strongly manipulating author. Even the title, like that of the earlier novel, *Small Ceremonies*, links a vague or weak initial adjective that normally would not arouse any special interest with a stronger noun which has overtones (or at least distant memories) of religion. The nouns have a formality usually denied by the adjectives, and this makes us aware of a creator intentionally starting with the weaker word.

The initial terse paragraph, both casual and authoritative, establishes the tone: "Several of the miracles that occurred this year have gone unrecorded" (13). Each of the six "miracles" begins with a date and an almost identical form of presentation, although after two very brief miracles, each new one receives a longer description. The first sets the pattern: "Example: On the morning of January 3, seven women stood in line at a lingerie sale in Palo Alto, California, and by chance each of these women bore the Christian name Emily" (13). While some readers will think more of coincidence than of miracles, others will stress the way, perhaps arbitrarily, that the "author" (for the narrator never receives distinguishing traits or past experiences and never explicitly refers to her[?]self) creates and arranges the examples. But the third miracle (dropping "Example") adds a different order of reality.

> On March 30 a lathe operator in a Moroccan mountain village dreamed that a lemon fell from a tree into his open mouth, causing him to choke and die. He opened his eyes, overjoyed at being still alive, and embraced his wife . . . she was dreaming . . . that a lemon tree had taken root in her stomach . . . she began to tremble . . . with happiness and intoxication . . . her face radiant. What he saw was a mask of happiness so intense it made him fear for his life. (13)

By now, the earlier convincing mimetic realism may seem to have become completely irrelevant. The "miracles" lie in the power of the creator's imagination and skill. To refuse (or fail) to delight in this exultant artifice would leave the reader incapable of enjoying this story.

Particularly deft in expressing another completely different relation of story-teller to material is the much more extended "Dolls, Dolls, Dolls, Dolls." Starting with a long unquoted letter she has received from a friend who was visiting a doll factory in Japan, the narrator then recalls how she herself was given one doll every year until she was ten. She goes on to describe a visit in the suburbs of Paris to "one of the finest archeological museums in Europe" (129) where her daughter insists that the pre-Christian icons might be dolls. The story-teller feels "sick with sudden inexplicable anger" (131) when her husband tries to correct the child, but then immensely relieved when he shrugs, smiles, and says, " 'You might be right. Who knows' " (131). The fourth section, corresponding to the final repetition in the title, presents a story in itself as the speaker and her sister share both recollections and a strange forgetfulness about their childhood. These lead the speaker to remember the terrible murder of a little girl, "ten years old, my age" (134) and especially her own horrible fears and attempts to cope with them for the rest of that summer. A battered old doll, Nancy Lynn, "protects" her (137), although "I knew she was lifeless. . . . Human love, I saw, could not always be relied upon. There would be times when I would have to settle for a kind of parallel love" (137).

In this vivid story, close to a meditation, Shields presents us with nothing that could not be factually or autobiographically true. In this example of an increasingly widespread sub-genre, she achieves a brilliant success, comparable to the best stories of the unheralded master, James McConkey. The work can be considered as memoir, as autobiography, or as fiction. But unlike the stories of McConkey or the gripping monologue *No Place Like Home* by Shane McCabe (the outstanding critical and popular favourite at the 1990 Winnipeg Fringe Festival), "Dolls" would be in no way diminished if its facts were no more literally true than those of "Mrs. Turner" or of "Dying for Love." Shields achieves here a convincing effect of autobiographic truth in which we never go outside the thoughts and the memories set off in the extremely credible narrator, who might well be the author. We read the story *as if* its events and feelings were true.

To discuss the *oeuvre* of Carol Shields in mid-career would require consideration not only of her 11 books, including novels, stories, poems, and a play, but also of her uncollected reviews. Instead, by focusing upon four stories—especially through extensive quotations—we can see how central to her work is the range of tones rather than of subject matter or of location. We can often hear an effective speaking voice, especially in its needling humour. We always find carefully crafted comments upon characters and their situations, but how often do we consider these apart from our awareness of their construction? When her command of various tones results in our immediate assent, we will often subsequently find how our noticing the artifice increases the vividness and the resonance of the scene. Readers may well differ in deciding whether the word "miracle" should apply to extreme coincidence or to the comeback of a losing player or to the creation suddenly bursting out from unpromising material. But we should all share the delight, as we read, when, contrasting the initial description of Mrs. Turner's attire, we discover the exquisite tact of the final sentence in the story: "Oh, what a sight is Mrs. Turner cutting her grass, and how, like an ornament, she shines."

Running as sub-texts through this essay have been the varying relations of reader-response theory to the narrator and to the author. More overt have been the relations of the implied author (sometimes the "I") to the characters, the ideas they embody or express, and the events of the stories. Some of Shields' more intriguing resonances come if we now attend consciously to a sequence of relations leading from those internal ones we have discussed to those of the work to the reader. In "Mrs. Turner," for example, as we have seen, the reader is engaged from the first lines in a wide variety of ways. But the reader's retrospective engagement will prove quite unlike his/her initial response. At first, most of us may well share the views of the teen-age girls, the selfish ecologically minded neighbours, or the poet about Mrs. Turner—however little we may identify with those characters in other respects. By the end of the story, most of us will agree that Mrs. Turner is an ornament, for Shields has transformed this initially unattractive character through a final vision without mockery or condescension.

Some will not want to stop at this closure. Isn't the poet, especially, treated with mockery and condescension? However important or unimportant one feels one's answer is to this last question, readers of Carol Shields may suspect that she is—or was—prepared to write other stories about these other characters she has created—so that in the vision of the whole, mockery and condescension give way to compassion and celebration.

Works Cited

Shields, Carol. "Dolls, Dolls, Dolls, Dolls." *Various Miracles* 123-37.

__________. "Dying for Love." *Room of One's Own* 13.1/2 (July 1989): 60-68 and *West Coast Review* 23.3 (Winter 1989): 21-27. Rpt. in *Made in Manitoba: An Anthology of Short Fiction*. Compiled by Wayne Tefs. Winnipeg: Turnstone Press, 1990. 145-54.

__________. "Mrs. Turner Cutting the Grass." *Various Miracles* 18-27.

__________. *Small Ceremonies*. Toronto: McGraw-Hill Ryerson, 1976.

__________. *Various Miracles*. Don Mills: Stoddart Publishing Company, 1985.

__________. "Various Miracles." *Various Miracles* 13-17.

CONTRIBUTORS

David Arnason, a teacher, critic, poet, and prose-narrative and play writer, works out of St. John's College at the University of Manitoba, and is currently finishing a novel for Talonbooks.

Dennis Cooley is a teacher, critic, and poet at St. John's College, University of Manitoba, who is currently writing poetic and literary-critical discourses.

Debbie D'Aoust is enrolled in graduate studies in English and writes out of the University of Manitoba.

Charlene Diehl-Jones sings jazz and writes literary-critical discourse when not working on the final phase of a Ph.D. at the University of Manitoba.

Kenneth James Hughes teaches and writes about most things out of St. John's College at the University of Manitoba, and his *The Unfinished Body: Subjectivity and Discursive Formations* is due from Talonbooks in spring 1991.

Judith Owens energetically mixes mothering, teaching, writing, and the final phase of a Ph.D. in English at the University of Manitoba.

Birk Sproxton teaches, writes books and articles, and edits for a press he helped found out of Red Deer College, Alberta, from whence he regularly returns to his native Manitoba.

Margaret Sweatman, deep into Praxis, mixes mothering, studying, writing, and general living in Winnipeg, and is currently finishing a novel.

Wayne Tefs combines the teaching of sports and English and writes novels and critical discourse in the middle of a very busy schedule at St. John's-Ravenscourt School in Winnipeg.

Herb Weil teaches and writes out of the English Department at the University of Manitoba, of which Department he was formerly the Head.